THE FAILURE OF CORPORATE SCHOOL REFORM

Critical Interventions
Politics, Culture, and the Promise of Democracy
A Series from Paradigm Publishers
Edited by Henry A. Giroux, Susan Searls Giroux, and Kenneth J. Saltman

Twilight of the Social: Resurgent Publics in the Age of Disposability
By Henry A. Giroux (2011)

Youth in Revolt: Reclaiming a Democratic Future
By Henry A. Giroux (2012)

The Failure of Corporate School Reform
By Kenneth J. Saltman (2012)

THE FAILURE OF CORPORATE SCHOOL REFORM

KENNETH J. SALTMAN

Paradigm Publishers
Boulder • London

Copyright © 2012 by Paradigm Publishers

Published in the United States by Paradigm Publishers, 5589 Arapahoe Avenue, Boulder, Colorado 80303 USA.

Paradigm Publishers is the trade name of Birkenkamp & Company, LLC, Dean Birkenkamp, President and Publisher.

Library of Congress Cataloging-in-Publication Data

Saltman, Kenneth J., 1969–
  The failure of corporate school reform / Kenneth J. Saltman.
      p. cm.
  Includes bibliographical references and index.
  ISBN 978-1-61205-210-6 (pbk. : alk. paper)
  1. Privatization in education—United States. 2. Educational change—United States.
  3. Neoliberalism. I. Title.
  LB2806.36.S264 2012
  371.010973—dc23
                                                            2012009873

Printed and bound in the United States of America on acid-free paper that meets the standards of the American National Standard for Permanence of Paper for Printed Library Materials.

Designed and Typeset by Straight Creek Bookmakers.

16 15 14 13 12   5 4 3 2

CONTENTS

PREFACE AND ACKNOWLEDGMENTS

This book could have had another title, such as *The Theft of Public Schools: How Corporations and the Rich Are Ending U.S. Public Schooling*. Or, it could have been called *The New Two-Tiered System of Public Education: Privatized at the Bottom*. It could have even been called *Those Who Can, Sell; Those Who Can't, Sell For-Profit Education for Think Tanks*. Instead this book is called *The Failure of Corporate School Reform* for a few reasons.

First, after two decades of corporate school reforms, the evidence for what proponents of corporate school reformers say matters—namely, the evidence on test scores and costs—looks bad. Really bad. This book lays bare the ugly evidence. Privatizing and deregulating, and introducing "market competition" through "choice," have failed to do what proponents promised. As well, two decades after Chubb and Moe's justification in *Politics Markets and America's Schools* for privatization on the basis of reducing bureaucratic red tape in public schooling, this book illustrates that an entirely new privatized bureaucracy has been created by the forces of corporate school reform. Yet, the new bloated multi-level privatized bureaucracy is decidedly antidemocratic, being far less subject to public oversight and shared governance and instead shifting control and wealth to private moneyed interests.

Second, these promises of corporate school reform were premised on the declaration of a "failed" public school system. Such declaration of system "failure" was never credible, as the parts of the system that received high investment have always excelled, according to traditional measures of quality. The agenda all along has been to privatize and commodify schools in working-class and poor urban and rural communities. These schools and communities have been historically shortchanged, receiving about a third of the per-pupil investment of the best-funded public schools.

This book shows that if corporate school reform is a "success," it is a success in this regard: making kids into commodities for investors, pillaging public services in a stalled economy, and exacerbating the already record levels of inequality in wealth and income. Working-class and poor students have been made into investment opportunities for the richest Americans by being made pawns in the multi-billion-dollar industries in contracting, school management, test publishing, and database tracking. This profiteering grotesquely merges with draconian punitive and carceral forms of racialized and class-based bodily control, particularly in the schools of poor and working-class urban nonwhite students who are also subjected to anti-intellectual anticritical forms of teaching and learning.

In addition to the material and symbolic violence perpetuated on children, the tragedy is that American adults have turned their backs on the aspiration for educational equality, refusing to provide equal school funding, refusing to desegregate public schools, and refusing to allow an intellectual curriculum and critical pedagogies. While historically public schooling has been involved in reproducing a racialized class hierarchy, strengthening public schooling has to mean challenging this historical legacy by working toward racial and ethnic integration, equal funding, and a critical intellectual curriculum. Corporate school reform represents a profound failure to address the historical shortcomings of public schooling and instead exacerbates these aspects. Corporate school reform worsens racial segregation and funding inequalities, and it puts in place standardization, rote learning, and rigid disciplinary approaches to learning instead of fostering creative, critical pedagogical and dialogic forms of learning. So the title of the book turns the metaphor around. The problem is not that public schooling has failed but that corporate schooling has failed. And corporate school reform compounds the injuries resulting from the select ways public schooling has historically shortchanged working-class and poor citizens. Corporate school reform has not just failed at raising test scores and lowering costs but also has failed kids in terms of basic educational fairness. It has failed society with a misguided vision of what public schooling can offer everybody in a democracy.

I and others from the critical perspective have been writing about the corporatization of schooling for well over a decade. Yet, the extent to which public schools have come under attack by the forces of profiteering has only just become part of public discourse. The corporatization of schools has been publicized in documentaries and on TV in part because of the sustained propaganda efforts of those bankrolling it, such as venture philanthropists, corporate foundations, and media companies with direct financial interests in the corporate takeover of schools. As well, the backlash against the corporate takeover has received increasing public attention. Diane Ravitch, former assistant secretary of education under George H. W. Bush, has played a large part in bringing to national attention claims that her former opponents on the left had been making for a long time. Ravitch's book, *The Death and Life of the American School,* describes her conversion from right-wing think-tank privatization advocate to defender of public schools and teachers' unions and has been particularly compelling to liberals and the progressive media. Although her media blitz granted wider exposure to the evidence that corporate reforms were having negative effects in terms of scores and costs and "narrowing the curriculum," it shut out of the discussion some of the most important aspects of corporate school reform, including serious discussion about the extent to which cultural politics is at play in schooling, the extent to which schools function to reproduce a stratified labor force for a race to the bottom economy, and how the attack on public schooling is part of a broader neoliberal restructuring that is a form of class and cultural warfare waged by the rich on the rest.

The liberal criticism of corporate school reform, as I explain in Chapter 4, fails to address that schooling and its radical remaking is profoundly imbricated with broader economic and cultural struggles. A vision of public schooling for a more just, equal, and democratic global society cannot argue for strengthening public schools in the interests of shoring up American military and economic supremacy (Darling-Hammond) or more efficaciously transmitting the cultural cannon (Ravitch). Nor is it adequate to defend traditional community schools if they remain tied to a racially segregated system of real-estate wealth. Instead, any democratic criticism of corporate school reform needs to not simply defend public schools. It needs to seek to *remake* them in ways that accord with the values of a critical democratic society. That is, efforts for strengthening public schools need to champion pedagogical approaches that make central to teaching and learning how claims to truth secure particular forms of authority, how the making and circulation of knowledge have to be understood in terms of broader material and symbolic interests and contests, and how particular contexts and experiences need to be theorized in terms of the forces and structures that produce oppression, injustice, and violence. As well, proponents of strengthening public schools need to understand the public mission of public schools as involved in self and social reconstruction, the development of critical forms of agency, and collective efforts for community and global justice.

Moreover, as this book suggests, corporate school reform has to be seen in the context of a broader pillaging of the public sector by corporations and the rich in the past few decades. This pillaging has privatized not just public schools and universities but also public housing, public health care, public roads, the military, the airwaves, and the water we drink. As the last chapter argues, the global neoliberal restructuring of the economy and culture is not inevitable, nor is it the only vision possible. Recent scholarship on the commons and the Occupy movement open up new ways for critical education to imagine what schools can be about in a public democracy: not only fostering democratic social relations, civic participation, and critical pedagogical dispositions but also providing a place where students learn to enact alternatives to neoliberal capitalism. That is, schooling can be a formative culture whereby citizens learn how common labor can produce common benefit rather than individualized benefit.

Corporate school reform propaganda has entered into public discourse in the past two years through media but also through "astroturf" (fake grassroots) organizations that are heavily bankrolled by rich donors like Stand for Children and Students First, lavishly corporate-supported charter associations, the right-wing education think-tank machine, and venture philanthropies like the Gates, Broad, and Walton foundations. Yet, a backlash against corporate school reform has also entered public discourse and is rapidly growing at the local, state, and national levels, with increasing awareness and action by teachers, students, unions, and activists. Some students are walking out on standardized tests. Some union chapters, such as Chicago's Caucus of Rank and File Educators, have linked their vigorous defense of teachers and students to broader struggles against economic inequality, urban dispossession, and corporate influence. Protesters are occupying boards of education meetings, state capitols, and schools targeted for corporate-style "turnarounds." Independent education bloggers are often able to debunk the corporate school reform lies and manipulations at speeds and with reach that policy journals and books cannot often match. These are efforts and incidents that corporate media (nearly always aligned with corporate school reform) cannot ignore. Corporate school reformers have an affinity for business metaphors like "churn" and "creative destruction." This book aims to turn the metaphor of "creative destruction" around as well and to be an accelerant to the fire of opposition that has ignited against corporate school reform. What has to be planted in the ashes of the failed corporate model is a reinvigorated collective commitment to critical forms of public schooling that can be the basis for expanding genuine democracy throughout all institutions, the economy, and the culture.

I would like to thank editors Dean Birkenkamp and Jason Barry at Paradigm Publishers for their valuable input on the project and for being an absolute plea-sure to work with again. I also thank my friends and colleagues whose ongoing invaluable exchange informed various parts of the project, especially my wonder-ful friend and collaborator Robin Truth Goodman, whose regular exchange and generous feedback on the entire book was crucial. As always, my great friend Henry Giroux provided brilliant insights and inspiration on this project and beyond. Henry is nothing less than an international treasure whose academic and public influence is too great to be measured. To have the privilege of ongoing exchange with him and his friendship is the greatest honor I can think of. Big thanks go to my friend Alex Means, with whom I extensively discussed ideas in Chapter 3 on the new market bureaucracy in public education. Alex's generosity in sharing his keen insights from his ethnographic studies and theoretical reading proved invaluable in this project. Alex Molnar played an outsized role in Chapter 2, as it began as a policy brief for the National Education Policy Center and was subject to Alex's stringent demands and eagle eye. Others at the National Educa-tion Policy Center whose input was extremely valuable include William Mathis, Patricia Hinchey, the great Gary Miron (whose empirical studies of charters are unparalleled), and the downright heroic Susan Ohanian, as well as director Kevin Welner, whose path-breaking work on neo-vouchers is a far underrecognized aspect of the privatization agenda. Parts of Chapter 1 were developed through my talks on educational privatization in Louisiana for the Louisiana Board of El-ementary and Secondary Education and the Louisiana School Board Association, which were helpfully facilitated by Republican renegade and firebrand Tammy McDaniel—who also gave me a wonderful tour of the Delta. Thanks to graduate assistants Andie Thomalla, Mara O'Shea, Maria Ocasio, and Mallory Wessell for their research contributions. A number of other friends and colleagues provided valuable ongoing exchange, support, and inspiration, including Philip Kovacs, Wayne Ross, Donaldo Macedo, Pepi Leistyna, Christopher Robbins, Susan Searls Giroux, Josh Sheppard, David Gabbard, Joao Paraskeva, Sheila Macrine, Enora Brown, Stephen Haymes, Amira Proweller, Chris Murray, Deron Boyles, Trevor Norris, John Portelli, Megan Boler, Sandra Mathison, Kristen Buras, Noah Sobe, Lois Weiner, William Watkins, Jackson Potter, Sarah Hainds, Hugh McLean, Ian

XII PREFACE AND ACKNOWLEDGMENTS

McPherson, Susan Robertson, Hk Christie, Clayton Pierce, Noah Delissavoy, Richard Kahn, Julia Hall, Tony Carusi, Brad Porfilio, Lou Downey, Al Lingis, Noah Gelfand, Rob Isaacs, Jeff Truell, and Kevin Bunka.

Finally, thanks for the love and support of my daughter, Simone, and her mom, Kathy, to whom this book is dedicated with hope for the future.

CHAPTER ONE
THE FAILURE OF CORPORATE SCHOOL REFORM

In the United States, a corporate model of schooling has overtaken educational policy, practice, curriculum, and nearly all aspects of educational reform. While this movement began on the political right, the corporate school model has been heralded across the political spectrum and is aggressively embraced by both major parties. Corporate school reformers champion private sector approaches to reform including, especially, privatization, deregulation, and the importation of terms and assumptions from business, while they imagine public schools as private businesses, districts as markets, students as consumers, and knowledge as product. Corporate school reform aims to transform public schooling into a private industry nationally by replacing public schools with privately managed charter schools, voucher schemes, and tax credit scholarships for private schooling. The massive expansion of de-unionized, nonprofit, privately managed charter schools with short-term contracts is an intermediary step toward the declaration of their failure and replacement by the for-profit industry in educational management organizations (EMOs). EMOs extract profit by cutting teacher pay and educational resources while relying on high teacher turnover and labor precarity.[1] Corporate school reform seeks solutions to public problems in private sector ways, from contracting out schools and services, to union-busting, a wholesale embrace of numerical benchmarking and database tracking, and the modeling of schooling and administration on multiple aspects of corporate culture. Policy hawks make demands, for example, for teacher entrepreneurialism, or insist that students dress like retail chain workers and call school heads "CEO," or install corporate models of numerical "accountability" equating knowledge with cash and pay students for grades and teachers for test scores; or leaders play intricate Wall Street–style shell games with test performance to show rising "return on investment," or encourage teachers to assign students the task of crafting a resume for Benjamin Franklin. The examples are endless.

Despite the fact that corporate school reforms have expanded at an exponential speed, the dominant corporate school reforms have failed on their own terms. Such reformers have insisted on "accountability" through test scores and lowering costs, but it is precisely in reference to these accountability measures that corporate school reforms have failed. The failing policies that are being aggressively implemented nonetheless include contracting out management to privately managed charters or for-profit educational management organizations,[2] putting in place voucher schemes or neo-voucher scholarship tax credits,[3] expanding commercialism,[4] imposing corporate "turnaround" models on schools and faculty[5] that often involve firing entire faculties and administrations, reducing curriculum and pedagogy to narrow numerically quantifiable and positivist test-based forms, creating "portfolio districts" that imagine districts as a stock portfolio and schools as stock investments,[6] reorganizing teacher education and educational leadership on the model of the MBA degree,[7] and eliminating advanced degrees and certification in favor of pay-for-test-performance schemes such as value-added assessment.[8]

These corporate school reforms are deeply interwoven with commercial interests in the multi-billion-dollar test and textbook publishing industries, the information technology and database tracking industries, and the contracting industries.[9] The corporate sector has in the past decade positioned education in the United States as a roughly $600 billion per year "industry," ripe for takeover.[10] As directions for future economic growth are uncertain, public tax money in public services appears to corporations and the super-rich who are flush from decades of upward redistributions as tantalizing to pillage.[11] These upward redistributions of public wealth and governance are particularly obvious in Wisconsin and New Jersey as tax cuts for the super-rich and corporations and slush funds for business development are funded by de-funding public and higher education; attacking teacher pay, benefits, and unions; expanding privatization schemes including vouchers, charters, and tuition fee hikes; and shifting educational costs onto individual working-class and professional-class individuals. The same agenda is being enacted in Michigan, Indiana, Florida, Ohio, and Pennsylvania, to name but a few.

Increasingly, corporate education reform intersects with corporate media as media corporations push the agenda and media executives participate in both corporate school reform and a revolving door with school districts and media corporations (Joel Klein, Michael Bloomberg, Cathie Black, Fox, Microsoft, Bill Gates, and so on) increasingly targeting public schools to capture public tax dollars through for-profit education technology. Likewise, corporate consultants like McKinsey and A.T. Kearney expansively influence, direct, and draft corporate school policy and reform, promoting and profiting from public-private partnership schemes. Globally, the World Trade Organization, International Monetary Fund, and World Bank treat public education as a private consumable service, setting the stage to redistribute governance by imposing corporate trade rules on nation-states such as forcing them to allow for-profit foreign firms to compete in public "markets" with cheap imported teacher labor.[12] Such global governance architecture stands to expand privatized forms of educational development[13] and exploitable flexible teacher work as seen, for example, in the ways cheap Filipina teacher labor was imported into a radically corporatized New Orleans school system following Hurricane Katrina.[14]

Corporate school reform frames the problems and issues facing public schooling through the language and logic of business.[15] Consequently, it frames its own successes and failures in ideological terms that its proponents present as neutral and universally valuable. Students and parents become "consumers" of private educational services rather than public citizens; administrators become business managers, CEOs, and entrepreneurs rather than public servants dedicated to the public good; and teachers are reduced to being service deliverers of commodified units of knowledge rather than intellectuals charged with fostering in students the knowledge, skills, and dispositions necessary to link knowledge to broader social issues and struggles. That is, a crucial social cost of corporatization is the gutting of the development of public schooling that can foster critical citizenship, critical consciousness, and engaged public participation. At odds with the false neutrality and universality posited by corporate school reformers, critical education scholars insist on the inevitably political dimensions of public schooling. That is, knowledge, values, and ideological positions of different individuals and groups are struggled over through contests over the curriculum, pedagogy, and the organization of schools. Consequently, the practices of teachers, students, and other cultural workers are not only inevitably political but ideally ought to be reflectively enacted and guided by normative political and ethical referents that themselves are subject to ongoing theorization and revision.

Corporate school reform has failed on its own dubious terms. It has not succeeding in increasing student test scores, reducing costs, reducing bureaucracy that impedes efficiencies, or reducing the so-called achievement gap. But it has succeeded spectacularly in reframing the debates about education in the academic, policy, and public realms.

The extent to which corporate school reform has won public and policy discourse is exemplified by the fact that the same story is told whether from right-wing think tanks like Heritage, Hoover, the American Enterprise Institute (AEI), and Fordham or allegedly progressive ones like the Center for American Progress: for example, public schooling primarily serves the needs of business; public schooling is responsible for global economic competition; the possibility for individual fulfillment and opportunity is opened only through the corporatized school system organized by "competition" and "choice"; and educational attainment most importantly translates to mean individual inclusion into a corporate economy as a consumer and as a worker. The right-wing foundations, such as Heritage, Hoover, AEI, Fordham, and Manhattan, have origins with seed money from the richly endowed far-right Olin, Bradley, and Scaife foundations. Fellows from these organizations are a relatively tight-knit group of scholars and policy analysts who occupy prominent government and academic positions, employ a massive support staff, and mentor junior fellows for the future. The educational vision of these policy wonks is consistent with a broader vision to gut the caregiving roles of the state, to roll back the social spending and social programs created by the Roosevelt administration during the Great Depression, and to redefine public goods and services as private ones that can be either eliminated or handed over to rich investors and corporations.

The basic tenets of neoliberalism—unfettered market deregulation and privatization of public services—have since 2008 been utterly discredited by economists across the political spectrum. Yet, in U.S. education policy, the neoliberal trend expands seemingly unabated as both parties increasingly treat public schooling as if it has no other function than to serve economic ends, making workers and consumers toward the aim of concentrated capital accumulation and a global race to the bottom for suppressed wages. All aspects of Race to the Top demonstrate a perverted socialism for the rich along the lines of the 2008 financial bailouts. Billions of public dollars are being dangled in front of states to induce them to expand privatized and managerialist school reform including charter schools, cash for grades, turnarounds, and other schemes. Such revisions imagine historically neglected schools as private enterprises that need to be subjected to the "creative destruction" of private markets. As America's largest financial and automotive businesses are deemed "too big to fail" and rescued by future generations of debt servitude,[16] America's public schools are being set up to be declared "failed" and then replaced by allegedly competitive markets. If the current concentrated control over the EMOs is any indication of what can be expected in the future once universal public schooling can be redefined as a private industry subject to "creative destruction," a small number of massive companies like EdisonLearning, K12, and Imagine Schools Inc. will be able to dominate the industry and claim they too are "too big to fail." The precedent is, of course, the Edison Schools, which in 2002, when on the verge of a total stock collapse, was saved from failure by then sitting and future governors of Florida Jeb Bush and Charlie Christ, who used public money—the Florida Public School teacher retirement funds—to buy up the stock and take the company private. Incidentally, as it became difficult for Edison to expand, Tungsten and Newton were spun off to take advantage of for-profit educational contracting.

The crisis of neoliberal U.S. public schooling involves a profound abdication of commitment toward investing in public schools as a site for fostering democratic cultural and social renewal. In the context of an otherwise commercially saturated civil society, public schools are one of the very few common spaces in the United States that offer the potential for public deliberation over public values. As the new reforms concentrate governance control of charters under predominantly private business councils, narrow the meaning of education to standardized test performance, standardize curriculum through the 21st Century Skills and Common Core movements, and limit the possibilities of teaching as an intellectual and social endeavor to tactics of test preparation, the potential role of schools of fostering engaged democratic citizens is utterly crushed.

Educational management organizations focus on managing schools for profit. Ninety-four percent of EMOs are charter schools. As of 2008–2009, at least 95 EMOs were operating in 31 states, with 339,222 students and at least 733 schools, with nearly 80 percent of students in schools managed by the 16 largest EMOs. Major large companies include EdisonLearning (62 schools), the Leona Group (67), National Heritage Academies (57), White Hat Management (51), Imagine Schools Inc. (76), Academica (54), the rapidly growing virtual online school company K12 (24), and Mosaica Education (33).[17] The largest EMO in terms of number of students, the Edison Schools (now EdisonLearning), has been beset by numerous financial and accountability scandals that, as I explain in my book *The Edison Schools: Corporate Schooling and the Assault on Public Education*, have less to do with corrupt individuals than with the impositions of privatization and the social costs of public deregulation.

Major privatization initiatives also include market-based voucher schemes allowed by the U.S. Supreme Court in 2002 (*Zelman v. Harris-Simmons*) and implemented by the U.S. Congress in Washington, D.C., and in the Gulf region following Hurricane Katrina.[18] States such as Wisconsin used the financial crisis of 2008 and state budget crises that followed to expand vouchers and charters drastically while cutting educational spending on traditional public schools and limiting local tax used for public schools while also cutting corporate taxes. Education conglomerate companies such as junk bond felon Michael Milken's Knowledge Universe aim to amass a number of different education companies. These conglomerate companies hold a variety of for-profit educational enterprises, including test publishing; textbook publishing; tutoring services; curriculum consultancies; educational software development, publication, and sales; toy making; and other companies.[19]

In the United States, the Elementary and Secondary Education Act ("No Child Left Behind") has fostered privatization by investing billions of public dollars in the charter school movement, which is pushing privatization with over three-quarters of new for-profits being opened as charters. No Child Left Behind (NCLB) also requires high-stakes testing, "accountability," and remediation measures that shift resources away from public school control and into control by test and textbook publishing corporations and for-profit remediation companies. As well, NCLB's supplemental educational services (SES) provision required for-profit remediation of low scores rather than investment in public schools needing help.

For-profit EMOs that are private school management companies are only one part of the private takeover of schools themselves. Nonprofit charters are premised on injecting a healthy dose of "market competition" into schooling, forcing schools to compete against each other for students and letting those that do not raise scores "go out of business." Despite the business rhetoric of competition, since their inception charters have relied disproportionately on grants and philanthropic donations (the Gates Foundation poured billions into charters) and now increasingly on government incentives and one-time payouts. In the Recovery School District in Louisiana, charters are receiving roughly double ($15,000) the per-student money of schools in the Orleans Parish, yet in traditional measures of student achievement compared by rate of improvement, the Recovery School District lags. The major academic national studies of charters find that they on the whole do worse than traditional public schools in traditional measures of student achievement.[20] It is important to realize that in the past decade charters have gotten unending political support from the zealous, organized, and richly funded charter movement with national and state charter lobbying groups such as state charter school associations and from Washington think tanks like Fordham, AEI, Hoover, and Heritage, but also financial support from the so-called venture philanthropies,[21] especially the Gates and Broad foundations, the New Schools Venture Fund, and the Charter School Growth Fund, all of which aim to replace public schooling with a national "market" in education.

Despite starting as a grassroots movement for innovative, independent, and alternative school models, the now-dominant corporate model of the "venture philanthropists" has emphasized "replicating" traditional school models and rigid approaches to learning that stand to create not innovation but rather homogeneous McEducation. The instability and unsustainability of charters comes in part from the fact that the extra money can and will dry up both from these philanthropies and from the government. When this happens, charters will eventually go "out of business," but not before doing all they can to cut costs to survive. Such cost-cutting has historically included displacing and underpaying local experienced teachers; hiring inexperienced teachers and burning them out while their salaries are low; using inexpensive, inexperienced Teach for America teachers and uncertified teachers, and relying on alternative certification;[22] union-busting; manipulating test scores; importing cheap teachers from overseas; counseling or pushing out special-needs students and English language learners to raise test scores; and contracting the running of schools to for-profit management companies.

Charters are often public in name but not in practice. Charters shift governance to unelected councils dominated by business people, and these councils redistribute decisions about schools away from public community control. They subcontract to private for-profit companies that drain public funds and can maintain financial secrecy away from public oversight. They introduce new educational inequalities under the guise of freedom of "choice" as they favor those citizens with the most money, social networks, and cultural savvy to game the school selection process. Charters also drain public resources as schools compete with each other to draw parents by spending effort and money on public relations

Myths and Realities About Charter Schools

Myths:

- They outperform traditional public schools in terms of traditional test-based performance (a myth repeated by Chicago mayor and former Obama chief of staff Rahm Emanuel).
- They cut through bureaucratic red tape to foster cost efficiencies.

Realities:

- Only 17 percent outperform traditional schools on tests while 37 percent do worse and 46 percent are on par. (These statistics for Chicago are nearly identical nationally.)[1]
- They cost more for administration relative to traditional counterparts while spending less on instruction.[2]
- They exacerbate racial segregation.[3]
- They rely on unstable private funding and concentrated private governance.[4]
- They result in the dismantling of democratically elected local school councils.[5]
- They de-unionize schools, resulting in higher teacher turnover and more inexperienced teachers.[6]
- They are incentivized to push out and keep out higher resource-intensive and lower scoring students.
- They contract with for-profit managers who skim resources out of the educational process.[7]
- They set the stage for further wide-scale privatization and instability by creating "churn" or "creative destruction."[8]
- Despite the early intention for charters to have alternative and independent models, the concentrated funding from the venture philanthropists (Gates and Broad) pushes the development of a narrow range of homogenous models that can be "replicated" and "scaled up."[9]

1. S. Banchero, "Daley School Plan Fails to Make Grade," *Chicago Tribune,* January 17, 2010, p. 1; D. Humphrey, V. Young, K. Bosetti, L. Cassidy, E. Rivera, H. Wang, S. Murray, and M. Wechsler,

and advertising that could be spent on teachers, books, and schools. Charters imagine students economically as workers and consumers, and consequently they overemphasize high-stakes tests, which in turn pushes schools to treat knowledge as something that students consume and regurgitate rather than fostering the kinds of public education that prepares students to think critically about the world they inhabit and to learn to act as citizens with others to change it for the better. Charters fail to address the problems of racial segregation and white flight, becoming complicit with the abandonment of the democratic aspirations

Renaissance Schools Fund-Supported Schools: Early Outcomes, Challenges, and Opportunities, Menlo Park, CA: SRI International, 2009, available at http://policyweb.sri.com/cep/publications/RSF_FI-NAL_April_15v2 .pdf. See also the studies listed in endnote 20.

2. G. Miron and J. L. Urschel, *Equal or Fair? A Study of Revenues and Expenditure in American Charter Schools,* Boulder, CO, and Tempe, AZ: Education and the Public Interest Center and Education Policy Research Unit, 2010, retrieved May 9, 2011, from http://epicpolicy.org/publication/charter-school-finance.

3. G. Miron, J. L. Urschel, W. J. Mathis, and E. Tornquist, *Schools Without Diversity: Education Management Organizations, Charter Schools, and the Demographic Stratification of the American School System,* Boulder, CO, and Tempe, AZ: Education and the Public Interest Center and Education Policy Research Unit, 2010, retrieved May 9, 2011, from http://epicpolicy.org/publication/schools-without-diversity.

4. K. J. Saltman, *Urban School Decentralization and the Growth of "Portfolio Districts,"* Boulder, CO, and Tempe, AZ: Education and the Public Interest Center and Education Policy Research Unit, 2010, retrieved May 9, 2011, from http://nepc.colorado.edu/publication/portfolio-districts.

5. Pauline Lipman and David Hursh, "Renaissance 2010: The Reassertion of Ruling-Class Power Through Neoliberal Policies in Chicago," *Policy Futures in Education* 5, 2 (2007); Kenneth J. Saltman, *Capitalizing on Disaster: Taking and Breaking Public Schools,* Boulder, CO: Paradigm, 2007.

6. Liz Brown and Eric Gutstein, "The Charter Difference: A Comparison of Chicago Charter and Neighborhood High Schools," Collaborative for Equity and Justice in Education, University of Illinois–Chicago, College of Education, February 17, 2009, available at www.uic.edu/educ/ceje/resources.html.

7. G. Miron and J. L. Urschel, *Equal or Fair? A Study of Revenues and Expenditure in American Charter Schools,* Boulder, CO, and Tempe, AZ: Education and the Public Interest Center and Education Policy Research Unit, 2010, retrieved May 9, 2011, from http://epicpolicy.org/publication/charter-school-finance.

8. K. J. Saltman, *Urban School Decentralization and the Growth of "Portfolio Districts,"* Boulder, CO, and Tempe, AZ: Education and the Public Interest Center and Education Policy Research Unit, 2010, retrieved May 9, 2011, from http://nepc.colorado.edu/publication/portfolio-districts; P. Hill, C. Campbell, and D. Menefee-Libey, *Portfolio School Districts for Big Cities: An Interim Report,* Seattle: Center on Reinventing Public Education, University of Washington, 2009; Andy Smarick "The Turnaround Fallacy," *Education Next* 10, 1 (2010). Smarick suggests that public schools should be thought of as private businesses competing against one another and, most important, that the "advantage" of charter schools is that they can be easily closed and replaced with other privatized solutions.

9. Kenneth J. Saltman, *The Gift of Education: Public Education and Venture Philanthropy,* New York: Palgrave Macmillan, 2010.

of the civil rights movement. As the Democratic Party steals the educational reform agenda from the Republicans, the political right is organizing to support charters in the short run in order to declare them as a failed experiment and set the stage for radically expanded educational privatization for the long run. That is, charters set the stage for future school privatizations by for-profit companies by being subject to closure. How has that worked out nationally, specifically in post-Katrina Louisiana, which has been an experiment in corporate school reform gone wild?

Caroline Roemer Shirley, head of the Louisiana Association of Public Charter Schools, attacked my public lecture in Rayville, Louisiana, in which I discussed how educational privatizers are capitalizing on disaster, the post-Katrina privatization onslaught, and the centrality of charters to privatization.[23] Shirley praises as "reputable" and "successful" EdisonLearning and SABIS, which are for-profit charter schools operating in Louisiana. As I discuss in my book *The Edison Schools,* as the largest-ever experiment in privatization, Edison overworked teachers, misreported earnings, misreported test scores, counseled out low-scoring students, cheated on tests to show high performance to potential investors, and, as it approached bankruptcy time and again, revealed just how precarious and unaccountable market imperatives can be when applied to education. SABIS has been accused of not just low enrollments but paying noncompetitive teacher salaries because of the need to draw off profits for investors. The relatively small number of for-profit charters relative to nonprofit charters owes much to the failures of several for-profit charters in post-Katrina Louisiana, including Mosaica Education, the Leona Group, and EdFutures Inc.

An accusation that plagued Edison in local districts around the country was: if Edison is supposed to bring the efficiencies and cost-cutting of the private sector to schooling, then why, as the editor of the Wichita, Kansas, *Eagle* asked, "does the model look so much like plain old panhandling?" The point not to be missed—and one that applies very much today in Louisiana—is that if business models of "efficiency," "competition," and "choice" work so well, why are the charter schools not getting the same per-pupil funding as the traditional public schools against which they are allegedly competing?

Creative Destruction

Despite the frequently heard claims about evidence-based reforms, the goal of the corporate school movement is *not* to improve public education; rather, it is to replace public education with a privatized national system of schools competing for scarce public dollars, regularly going out of business and allowing other profit-seekers to try their hand at running schools for profit. The privatization advocates call this "creative destruction" or "churn" and make little secret of their long-term vision. For example, Andrew Smarick of the Fordham Foundation and the American Enterprise Institute criticizes the Obama administration's emphasis on school turnarounds and explains that the problem with turnarounds is that they do not readily do what charters set the stage for: closing public schools. He writes that

> The beginning of the solution is establishing a clear process for closing schools. The simplest and best way to put this into operation is the charter model. Each school, in conjunction with the state or district, would develop a five-year contract with performance measures. Consistent failure to meet goals in key areas would result in closure.... Chartering has demonstrated clearly that the ingredients of healthy, orderly churn [creative destruction] can be brought to bear on public education.[24]

It is a mistake to think that school privatization is a Republican Party or Democratic Party issue. Both candidates in the 2008 presidential election spoke of the need to inject "competition" and "choice" into the education system. In the fall of 2009, the American Enterprise Institute, which is a leading pro-privatization think tank with a Republican Party orientation, teamed up with the Center for American Progress, led by Bill Clinton's chief of staff and Barack Obama's transition head John Podesta, to issue a report called "Leaders and Laggards: A State-by-State Report on Educational Innovation." The report came out as Race to the Top was finalized so that each state could know where it stood in relation to the desired reforms of Race to the Top, which follows much the same rationale of No Child Left Behind. Race to the Top dangles money in front of states to enjoin them to expand charter schools, tie teacher evaluation and merit pay systems to standardized test scores, and encourage local districts to dismiss entire staffs of thousands of "failing" schools. Although both political parties see education like business, the difference is that the Democratic Party sees privatization strategies as a tool for public school improvement. The thinking here is similar to that of the health care debates. A big dose of private sector competition should be injected into the public system, and the public schools should be forced to compete with private providers in the form of charters. For the political far right, the public system has failed and charters are an interim measure on the way to ending public education and replacing it with publicly funded private schooling. What the advocates for charters who want to strengthen public education do not seem to realize is that once traditional public schools are transformed into charters, they are easy to close and replace with private providers. The push for privatization is based not on evidence but rather on ideology and profit seeking.

In my 2007 book *Capitalizing on Disaster: Taking and Breaking Public Schools*, I showed how natural and human-made disasters are being used to implement school privatization policies that could not be put in place through standard political means. I detailed the ways that Hurricane Katrina was used to put in place preformulated plans for no-bid contracting, to expand turnaround consulting, to create the largest experiment in vouchers to date, to require data reporting from the public sector to be used by the private sector, and, most significantly, to create the largest and most aggressive experiment in dismantling an entire public school district—firing all the teachers, concentrating control over hiring of teachers and administrators under a single CEO, and replacing the former public district with a largely privatized network of charter schools.

I argued in *Capitalizing on Disaster* that what was afoot in the post-Katrina Gulf Coast needed to be understood as part of a broader trend to declare educational institutions as "failed" or as "disaster areas" to justify radical unproven experiments—specifically, radical experiments with a business approach to school reform. Rather than seeing such approaches as a marginal phenomenon, we ought to understand this as a dominant trend. The declaration of "disaster" as a reason for selling off public schools to private companies is found not just in the Gulf Coast but also is at the core of Arne Duncan's corporate-led Chicago school reform Renaissance 2010. Renaissance 2010 closed 60 schools and opened 100 privatized, de-unionized charters. As well, the educational reconstruction in post-invasion Iraq attempted to install charter schools there with multi-million-dollar profits for educational contractor Creative Associates International Inc. No Child Left Behind also acted aggressively to promote charter schools and required extensive use of for-profit supplemental educational services (SES) contractors, as well as putting in place adequate yearly progress (AYP) requirements for continual test-based increases that are designed to declare public schools as failed and ripe for closure and privatization in the future.

When I finished writing *Capitalizing on Disaster* in 2006 it had only been six months since Katrina hit New Orleans. Paul Vallas, a career accountant, had previously served as "CEO" of Chicago Public Schools and Philadelphia Public Schools and was just beginning as "CEO" of the Recovery School District in New Orleans. I was familiar with Vallas's work from Chicago as he implemented a strategy known as reconstitution, involving the firing of all the faculty and staff of a school and then swapping this workforce with that of another school (this practice, now called turnaround, continued throughout Arne Duncan's tenure and continued under Ron Huberman in Chicago. It is now being nationalized through Race to the Top). I was also familiar with Vallas because as I was working on my book *The Edison Schools*, Vallas attempted to have the for-profit company take over the running of the Philadelphia schools. Public outrage ensued, leading to a stock and capital crisis for the Edison Schools that culminated in the publicly traded company having its stock bought back. This cast a great deal of suspicion on Vallas's penchant for the radical privatization agenda.

While post-Katrina New Orleans was a model for radical neoliberal restructuring, Vallas is hardly the only master of disaster. The attacks and privatizations of public education in Wisconsin by Scott Walker, in New Jersey by Chris Christie, and in Indiana and Michigan in 2011 followed a very established game plan.[25] As a full-page color ad in Connecticut's right-wing *Yankee Institute* put it in 2005 in the Heartland School News, when the real estate bubble bursts and public education "costs soar relative to home values" in rich communities, wrote Executive Director Lewis Andrews, "savvy reformers will be prepared to make the case for school vouchers in all communities."

I want to emphasize that the issue here is not whether Vallas or other advocates of corporate school reform are good or bad people, well-intentioned or malicious; nor should we be trying to understand what is going on here as principally a matter of rare and exceptional acts of corruption—as real as corruption may be when it comes to no-bid contracts, real estate deals, and other profiteering tied to charters, or the cozy network of a small number of connected investors, policy experts, and politicians. It is also a mistake to think that the primary problem with corporate school reform is about something called "quality schooling" and simply trying new or different approaches to efficacious educational delivery. In this view, privatization is just a strategy or method we can use to see if we can improve this thing we assume we agree on called quality.

Instead of getting sidetracked by bad intentions and corruption it is crucial for the public to grasp that what is at stake in corporate school reform debates is a basic commitment to public education or a basic commitment to destroy it. I want to emphasize that privatization advocates have made up their minds that public education has failed. And the declaration of a failed public system is part of the ideological core of the privatization agenda. It is part of a series of interconnected business metaphors wrongly applied to public schooling including choice, monopoly, competition, consumers, and accountability that frame public schooling as a private business. The educational policy debates are now trapped in this framing, making it difficult to assert crucial democratic educational values including equality, fairness, justice, care, intellect, and the public good, to name a few.

In 2004, Bill Gates, who has championed charter schools far more aggressively than anyone else, appeared before the National Governors Association and gave a speech, a version of which was reprinted in multiple newspaper op-ed columns. Gates stated that "Our high schools are obsolete. By obsolete, I don't just mean that they're broken, flawed or under-funded, although I could not argue with any of those descriptions. What I mean is that ... even when they work exactly as designed, our high schools cannot teach our kids what they need to know."

"This is an economic disaster," he concluded, one that is ruining children's lives and "is offensive to our values."[26]

Likewise, Pete DuPont of the Lynde and Harry F. Bradley Foundation (a major funder of voucher projects) described the public school system as "awful," the worst thing the government does in America, and as "collectivism" that could be remedied by creating a market in education, and again by treating students and parents as consumers of private education. Similarly, Bruno Manno, who has served on the board of Fordham and as a senior associate at the Casey Foundation, wrote in the Hoover Institution–published *Primer on America's Schools* that "the present school enterprise is not just doing poorly, but is incapable of doing much better because it's intellectually misguided, ideologically wrong-headed, and organizationally dysfunctional."[27]

The declaration of the "failure" of public schooling forms the backbone of the privatization agenda. In my prior work, I have elaborated on the destructive implications of describing public schools and public goods generally as private goods.[28] I have emphasized that terms such as "failure," "choice," and "competition" (as well as "consumers," "efficiency," and "monopoly") are part of a broader long-standing neoliberal agenda[29] that extends far beyond education: misrepresenting public goods as private consumables, replacing the collective purpose of general welfare with the misguided terminology of profit accumulation, and portraying citizenship as consumerism.

Public school privatization and corporate school reform more broadly needs to be understood as an expression of neoliberal economic doctrine and ideology that is alternately known as neoclassical economics or market fundamentalism and is, in fact, a form of conservatism. At its most basic, neoliberal economic doctrine calls for privatization of public goods and services and the deregulation of state controls over capital, as well as trade liberalization and the allowance of foreign direct investment. As an ideology, neoliberalism aims to eradicate the distinction between the public and private spheres, treating all public goods and services as private ones. It individualizes responsibility for the well-being of the individual and the society, treating persons as economic entities—consumers or entrepreneurs—and it has little place for the role of individuals as public citizens or the collective public responsibilities of democracy. Within the purview of neoliberal ideology, the state can only be bureaucratically encumbered and inefficient, and the market naturally tends toward efficiency and effectiveness. Despite the antipathy to the state, neoliberals aim to shift the use of the state from its care-giving roles to its repressive ones.[30]

Since the early 1990s, neoliberal ideology has taken hold with a vengeance in education. This has involved describing public schooling as a business: students as "consumers," schools ideally needing to "compete" against one another, this competition driving up "efficient delivery," administrators described as "entrepreneurs," and schools needing to be "allowed to fail" "just like in business." (We should suppose this "allowed to fail" logic doesn't apply to the banking or automotive industries.) "High stakes" standardized testing and standardization of curriculum have been utterly central to the neoliberal education agenda in part because of the ways they treat knowledge as a commodity (abstract, allegedly neutral, numerically quantifiable units) to be produced by experts, delivered by teachers, and consumed by students. The critical and dialogic dimensions to learning and teaching are denied in this view that treats education as indoctrination of the "right knowledge." In the neoliberal perspective, this anticritical view of knowledge and learning is labeled "student achievement." The metaphorizing of public education in the language of the market has confused the private enterprise of profit accumulation with the public and civic purposes of public education.

Within the neoliberal view of education, declarations of "failure" have more than one function. As a rhetorical strategy, they make it seem as though the fault for low scores has to do with the low merits of students and the underperformance of teachers rather than excessive standardization, financial pressures on school systems, over-strained parents, economic disadvantages, racial discrimination, or the over-bureaucratization of knowledge. They thus redefine public schooling as private enterprise, and they naturalize private enterprise as the cure to public school "failings." As they conflate public and private sectors, they conceal how different levels of public investments result in different levels of educational quality and reflect historical inequalities in public investment.

The neoliberal declaration of a "failed system," which relies on the metaphor of business failure, is selectively deployed and is racially and class coded. It is not leveled explicitly against rich, predominantly white communities and public schools for which high levels of historical investment and the benefits of cultural capital have resulted in high achievement, traditionally defined. Rather, the declaration of "system failure" is leveled against the working class and the poor, predominantly nonwhite urban communities and schools. As such, it misattributes educational inequalities and shortcomings to the public sector rather than to the private sector. In the United States, the private sector bears responsibility for school underfunding as corporations capture public wealth through tax policies while not contributing to public school funding that provides their future workforce. As well, professional-class and ruling-class citizens at the helm of the private sector fight to maintain a radically unequal system of funding that links wealth to schooling through property taxes. Additionally, private sector forces such as the National Association of Manufacturers and the Business Roundtable have historically played a central role in engineering educational inequality.[31] The declaration of the "failed" public system has been widely used recently to push privatization. For example, as Paul Vallas and Arne Duncan in Chicago pushed the neoliberal approach through first "reconstitution" and then the Renaissance 2010 plan, the endlessly repeated suggestion has been that the public sector has "failed," and now it is "time to give the market a chance." The market, however, got a chance when the business sector influenced and shaped school reform and policy in Chicago for over a hundred years prior to Renaissance 2010 to the effect of defunding the urban system, fostering racial segregation and white flight to the suburbs, where marginally higher property taxes fund a nearly fourfold higher education expenditure per pupil. As Ben Joravsky has detailed in his exposé of tax increment financing zones, or TIFs, in the past couple of decades the urban tax base under Mayor Richard Daley was skimmed to shift money for schools into business slush funds.[32] The neoliberal solutions of union-busting, privatization, the idealization of deregulation in the form of charter schools, the idealization of competition and choice, the business-led reform, and the implementation of "turnarounds" as seemingly innovative solutions actively deny the ways in which the public system has a long history of business-led engineered failure, not to mention a history of unequal resource distribution by being tied to property wealth.[33]

So, when Gates, DuPont, Manno, Finn, and the countless others declare the "failure" of public schooling as potentially causing a broader economic crisis for the United States in the world, they are calling for a turn to the private sector to redress the problems that too much private sector involvement in education created in the first place. Moreover, these business tycoons and ideologues misrepresent their desire for an educated workforce where workers would compete in the global economy as a universally valuable vision rather than a class-specific one that largely benefits those who own and control capital. Such logic promotes that the public sector should subsidize job training and job preparation for the corporate sector, but that the corporate sector should not have to pay for it through taxes. Subjugating the public purposes of public schooling to primarily that of making competitive workers for the global economy presumes that the public interest is principally served by engaging in the global race to the bottom, fostered by the neoliberal vision of trade deregulation and public sector privatization. Privatizers openly talk about U.S. students ideally becoming workers who will compete for scarce jobs against workers from poorer nations. Values of worker discipline, docility, and submission to authority are injected into the corporate school vision as they represent the ideal of the disciplined, docile, and submissive bottom tier of the workforce. This view of the national education system, serving the interests of capital in a global economy, is at odds with the public interest that would be better served by a critical pedagogy. Critical pedagogy would let students build the tools of social criticism and develop as critical intellectual citizens who can learn to govern themselves and others, and who can deliberate on shared values beyond the shallow imperatives of consumerism and the desperate scramble for a shrinking pool of jobs.

"Value-Added" Assessment: Tool for Improvement or Educational "Nuclear Option"?

One of the most significant and destructive corporate school reforms is value-added assessment (also referred to as value-added models). To many, value-added assessment appears to be a new and promising educational innovation. The idea of value-added assessment involves measuring the changes over time in student test scores and attributing these changes to a teacher. If students score higher on a standardized test relative to the prior year, then the teacher is teaching well or "adding value" to the student. If the student test scores decline or do not improve relatively, then the teacher is not "adding value." The *Los Angeles Times* in August 2010[34] suddenly gave value-added assessment national prominence by publishing its own analysis of "value added" applied to the L.A. public school teachers' test improvement performance. The Obama administration has aggressively embraced it, making states' eligibility for $4.35 billion in competitive federal

Race to the Top grants contingent on states linking teacher evaluation to student test data. The growing enthusiasm over value-added assessment, however, belies what is actually a damaging policy for public education. Value-added assessment promises, rather, to dismantle teachers' unions, to de-intellectualize teachers' jobs, to refashion schools according to corporate-profit-making initiatives, and to burn out experienced teachers at ever faster rates. What its proponents fail to realize is that "value added" contributes to the destruction of public education by (1) participating in a broader corporate reform scheme of privatization; and (2) objectifying knowledge, or turning knowledge into "things," that is, units that can be measured, compared, and transmitted at the expense of genuine learning.

"Value added" is attractive to supporters because it appears to offer an objective measure of teacher performance that can be numerically quantified and tracked while also seeming to promise the ability to distill out from the data those teaching methods that result in higher test scores. The dream for proponents is to identify those methods, those teacher behaviors that raise test scores and then require teachers to adopt those allegedly successful methods. Additionally, "value added" promises to "out" those teachers who do not sufficiently raise test scores, thereby putting pressure on teachers and administrators to raise scores and especially putting pressure on teachers' unions by suggesting that firing, job security, and pay be linked not to professional review, tenure, advanced degrees, and seniority but rather to student test score improvement or decline. In fact, proponents are using it to transform university teacher preparation programs by considering the test score outcomes of school kids to determine which teacher education programs produce teachers who "add the most value." In other words, the value of an education professor who prepares future teachers would be measured by teaching candidates' future students' future test scores. There is no place in this view for pedagogical theory, learning tools to interpret different pedagogical contexts, or learning how to understand how schooling relates to broader social struggles, structures, and contested values.

Although value-added assessment may seem like a new idea to most Americans, the idea came out of Tennessee in the early 1990s and was viewed skeptically in academic and policy circles for nearly two decades. From then until now, there has been relatively little peer-reviewed empirically based research supporting or challenging the implementation of it, with the contentious debate focusing universally on the technical and methodological problems of the approach.[35] Early versions of value-added models were notoriously flawed; yet, recent alleged advances in the statistical modeling[36] have bolstered its appeal with those who accept its basic premise, especially standardized test–based measures of learning. Meanwhile, the financial incentivizing of the idea by the Obama administration, educational philanthropists like Gates and Broad,[37] long-standing drumbeating from right-wing foundations, and now the popularity from the *Los Angeles Times* analysis has given "value-added assessment" sudden prominence.

Yet, there has been a great deal of criticism of the idea in both academia and the popular press.[38] Some of the more damning criticisms have pointed to how "value-added assessment" attributes to a single teacher the teaching done by several teachers, including tutors (now more prevalent than ever with the supplemental educational services provision of No Child Left Behind). Critics have also suggested that "value added" treats test scores as the best and indeed only valuable measurement of student learning. Hence, value-added assessment is seen to share the same deficits of NCLB (which, despite the extreme emphasis on standardized testing, did not result in higher scores). It is criticized for over-emphasizing standardized testing at the expense of more holistic assessments and pedagogical approaches that account for and encourage student understanding (particularly in relation to nonquantifiable types of knowledge, like humanities and arts learning). It is also criticized for narrowing the curriculum, for encouraging teachers to "teach to the test" and compromise meaningful lessons for test preparation sessions.

Even those most sympathetic to the idea have espoused concerns about the technical limitations of value-added assessment. Writing in the *Wall Street Journal*,[39] Carl Bialik, the "Numbers Guy," points out that (1) "a large proportion of teachers who rate highly one year fall to the bottom of the charts the next year"; (2) "good teachers aren't easy to identify this way. For one thing, students are not always assigned to teachers randomly. A teacher getting more than his/her share of students who learn slowly because of his/her knack for helping them might be penalized at the end of the year"; and (3) small sample sizes (a class of 15–20 students in a year) yield unreliable analyses with the Department of Education, which estimates that even in three years of data, "one in four teachers is likely to be misclassified because unrelated variables creep in." Despite the seemingly dire methodological limitations of value-added assessment, Bialik nonetheless concludes that it looks like a useful tool relative to the alternative, namely subjective observations. The idea that Bialik and so many others find attractive is that the test scores offer an "objective" measure of a teachers' quality. Even liberal critics of value-added assessment, like Stanford education professor and Obama campaign advisor Linda Darling-Hammond, embrace this assumption of objectivity, suggesting that standardized testing can be a valuable tool but that the methodological limitations of value-added assessment mean that it should be combined with other forms of assessment, such as observation, not that the approach should be rejected outright. But this assumption of the objectivity of value-added assessment is a major fallacy.

Two criticisms of value-added assessment have been largely absent from the debate: (1) value-added assessment installs particular ideological and political values and ways of thinking while appearing to be value neutral, and it hence contributes to a dangerous anticritical/anti-intellectual approach to schooling that is thoroughly at odds with the best traditions of public education for citizen formation; and (2) in the current context of rapidly expanding public school privatization, market approaches to school reform, and virulent anti-unionism, value-added assessment contributes to the destructive trend toward the making of a new two-tiered educational system with an elite public upper tier and a privatized underfunded lower tier. This is having multiple effects: it is setting the stage for a de-skilled and low-paid private labor force; it makes profits for investors at the commodified bottom but leaves in place a highly unequal system; and it drains away much-needed public school resources to data crunching and test companies.

Whose Value? What Values?

On September 2, 2010, Arne Duncan's successor as "CEO" of the Chicago Public Schools, Ron Huberman, appeared before the City Club of Chicago and described value-added assessment as a tool that is beyond question or debate. He compared it to a car. You don't ask whether cars exist or not, he proclaimed; you just use one. Same with value-added assessment. All it measures is a change in performance over time. This, explained Huberman, would in the future be a central part of what he described as the "culture of performance" he plans for Chicago Public Schools (CPS). CPS has an office of performance management, and its vision for school improvement is to break down opposition to the enforcement of learning. In this perspective, every student can learn the mandated knowledge, and responsibility for learning is downwardly delegated to the individual teacher. The teacher is to learn how to diagnose obstacles to learning by employing a battery of tests, and ultimately, according to the CPS performance management website, the teacher will be able to overcome the "core" obstacles to learning. Unfortunately, these "core" obstacles do not include comprehending what makes learning meaningful, relevant, and motivating as opposed to deadening and uninteresting for students. While Huberman's enthusiasm to overcome obstacles to learning were no doubt well-intended, like most admirers of the value-added approach he fails to grasp that the core obstacles to learning are specifically *values* related.

There are two basically different ideas of educational value at play in this debate. For proponents of value-added assessment, standardized tests contain certain, verifiable, and numerically quantifiable knowledge. The tests are mistakenly thought to be objective. What is tragically denied in this view is the subjective aspect of test creation. Who made the test? What are their values, assumptions, class and cultural positions, and frames of reference for deciding what is true and what is of value to know? What to include and exclude from the test?

The obvious examples that highlight just how subjective are the allegedly objective material on standardized tests are the historical and reading exam passages that are inevitably coming from a particular vantage point (typically ones of political, military, and economic supremacy). Such reading exams reference, for example, the history of colonial conquest written by the victors rather than the victims, or the history of the production of soap that includes mention of advertising and marketing but nothing about the workers who made it or the racialized discourse that was used to promote its sale.[40] It is common to cite Howard Zinn's *People's History* as an antidote to the history of the powerful few, but too often these counter examples become the basis for claiming "test bias" that can be overcome if only the tests are tweaked to be made "less biased" and "more objective." But these are incoherent concepts because "less biased" still presumes a disinterested objectivity forged by removing subjective values, assumptions, and ideals. The crucial point is that ideological assumptions and framing values are *always* inevitably informing what is selected and taught. Better teaching makes these ideological assumptions and framing values more explicit rather than denying them so that the student can develop the capacity to interpret, analyze, and criticize claims to truth. These kinds of skills of interpretation give students the capacity not only to better and more critically learn socially valued traditions of knowledge but also to analyze and comprehend what they experience in their communities and in their lives, what they are being taught in academic literature, mass media, and popular culture, and even to produce new, inventive, and yet unimagined knowledge. Such knowledge is the basis not only for solving technical problems but dire social ones as well. Ultimately, such skills of interpretation are crucial to students learning how to analyze and address public problems such as poverty, inequality, and the radically undemocratic concentrations of wealth and political power in the United States and around the globe. Valuing learning as the struggle over values and meanings is not a fall to subjectivism. On the contrary, it is more scientific. As one of the greatest American philosophers, John Dewey, suggested, truths are arrived at through dialogue and debate; they are revisable and fallible as in science. Indeed, what "value added" assessment does is to wrap canonical dogma in a veneer of scientism. If you put a number on the test, then who can argue with numbers?

Some might concede that historical or reading passages do have an inevitably subjective dimension but not the hard sciences and math. Yet as Eric Gutstein, Robert Moses, Bill Tate, and many other critical math education scholars show, the ways that students learn math and science are profoundly political. The realization of the politics of math has implications for student motivation and whether a lesson is meaningful or unbearable. Gutstein teaches decimals and fractions to Latino middle school students in Chicago through lessons that deal with, for example, "driving while brown/driving while black"—engaging the racial profiling that many of his students have experienced in their city. He links students' experiences to the mathematical tools in order to help them better understand crucial public matters of inequality. Math becomes not merely academically valuable but promises to become a tool for students to confront injustice. The values and assumptions of such a lesson are as important as those, say, that teach what percentage of Laos remains littered with American munitions from the "secret bombing" during the Vietnam war wherein more bombs were dropped than in World War II. These bombs continue to kill on a daily basis and prevent agricultural and industrial development; the math lesson includes determining what percentage of Americans know this, and why. Another example of meaningful math is seen in calculating the percentage of the earth's species that are being killed off in a given year. Corporate school reform is premised on "global economic competition" that has no way of dealing with imminent ecological collapse. Yet, BP, the worst environmental polluting oil company, grasps just how political education is as it has been involved for seven years in creating the new environmental education standards and environmental curriculum for the state of California, rolled out in winter 2011 for grades K–12 in 1,000 school districts.[41]

What is at stake in education getting at crucial public values is nothing short of the survival of the planet. Educational reform cannot wait to make primary values coincide with global citizenship, universal prosperity, and ecological sustainability. On the contrary, pedagogical approaches and assessment strategies like value-added assessment prohibit what is taught in schools from being taken up in relation to the broader values and competing visions for the future informing the selection and teaching of that knowledge. To put it differently, public schools are places where matters of public importance must be publicly debated so that students can learn the dispositions of engaged citizenship. If we ask the question of what do the proponents of value-added assessment and other anti-intellectual reforms want from public schools, the inevitable and now omnipresent answer is a workforce capable of competing in the global economy. But this is an incoherent claim, as capital zooms around the world in the global race to the bottom for cheap, no-benefit, nonunionized labor to produce cheap, disposable consumer goods. American school kids should study hard, doing memorization for standardized tests so they can compete against low paid Chinese factory workers? Or are they competing against all of the Indian moto-taxi drivers with graduate degrees in information technology who can be found leaning against their seldom hired cabs from Mysore to Bangalore? As of this writing the United States is faced with an unemployment rate of about 10 percent (higher for youth and much higher for African Americans and Latinos), with 85 percent of college graduates moving back in with their parents. Value-added logic suggests that children should absorb facts to make them more employable even though they face a future of unemployment, or temporary, part-time, and unstable employment, even as both political parties agree to scale back the social safety net in order to maintain enormous corporate profits and tax benefits for the super-rich who benefit from such labor precarity.

Putting Value-Added Assessment in the Context of the Corporate Takeover of Public Schooling

Value-added assessment is being promoted in conjunction with a number of corporate education reforms including chartering and the linked continued expansion of private for-profit school managers (EMOs), corporate-style school turnarounds, scholarship tax credits (or neo-vouchers), standardized curriculum, the privatization of teacher education and educational leadership programs, and a frontal assault on teachers' unions. These efforts are being promoted by think tanks funded by corporate dollars in addition to venture philanthropies including the Gates, Broad, and Walton foundations, and they have been largely embraced by both political parties. For twenty years the business metaphors of choice and competition, consuming education, and corporate accountability have been invoked to reframe public education as a private consumable commodity. These corporate reforms have no way of dealing with the history of unequal public education other than to leave in place elite public schooling while commodifying and commercializing the bottom tier of public schooling that has historically shortchanged working-class people and people of color.

The corporate reforms address neither the apartheid state of American schooling nor the structural radical funding inequalities ($8,000 per pupil in Chicago and nearly four times that in the north suburbs) that stand alone in the industrialized world,[42] and they fail to increase the intellectual climate in schools. Instead, they set the stage for a more thoroughly privatized bottom tier of the public system in which public tax dollars are funneled to private for-profit companies who can (as is now conclusively shown by studies, as cited earlier) deliver nothing more than their public counterparts but often deliver less. Public schools for the working class, poor people, and people of color have long served as holding pens, often contributing to economic and political exclusion rather than ameliorating them, and they have kept youth out of the labor force. But despite the business metaphor that the public schools have failed and now it is time to give the market a chance, it must be recognized that the current failures of public education are a direct result of a century of business-led reforms (from the National Association of Manufacturers to the Business Roundtable to the local business groups like the Commercial Club of Chicago) and the linkage of public school investment to private wealth through property taxes. The latest corporate reforms—including charters, vouchers, contracting, and value-added assessment—do nothing to reverse these grievous ills historically affecting public schools, but they do make the most vulnerable kids into multi-billion-dollar opportunities for owners of test and textbook publishing companies, for-profit school management companies, charter operators, and information technology data manipulators.

By linking student test scores to teacher value, proponents of corporate school reform take dead aim at teachers' unions, which they accuse of standing in the way of reform. The numbers, they will claim, speak for themselves. As Lois Weiner reminds us, the unions do stand in the way of furthering the corporate school reform agenda that aims to turn teachers into low-paid delivery agents of prepackaged curriculum and preformulated scripted lessons. The destruction of teachers' work conditions and pay is a crucial prerequisite for maximizing owner profit in the business of running schools, essentially shifting public tax dollars away from working teachers and into the accounts of education investors. Teachers' unions and the broader public should take a hard line against the adoption of value-added assessment not only for the well-being of teachers but for the well-being of kids who benefit as well from a well-paid, qualified, and stable corps of teachers. And the society benefits by efforts to stave off the antipublic coordinated corporate reforms.

The Corporate Assault on Teacher Education

The push for value-added assessment is being coordinated with the growing movement to privatize or dismantle teacher education programs and to radically restructure them in anticritical and anti-intellectual ways. This movement seeks the removal of teacher education from higher education in the interests of decreasing labor costs and expanding the profits extracted from public schooling. Such efforts represent the upward redistribution of public school money to ruling- and professional-class people, an ideological redefinition of the purposes and roles of public schooling, and a broader project of what Giroux has termed public pedagogy. This ideological redefinition runs counter to the making of critical citizens and instead promotes the making of a society composed of either consumers or disposable populations.[43] The attack on teachers and teacher education as a form of public pedagogy represents a public assertion of a diminished conception of education that can only be seen in terms of its economic exchange value.[44]

The neoliberal remaking of K–12 schooling is inextricably bound up with efforts to privatize teacher education while eradicating its most emancipatory possibilities. This "marketplace" is oriented toward a vocational, de-professionalized vision of teaching as training for low-paid service work rather than as professional, critical intellectual[45] public work. This is why efforts to privatize teacher education are being promoted by the same rightists who seek to promote a slew of privatization initiatives that reduce teacher labor expenditures, minimize teacher control, and allow teacher labor to be exploited for profit. Such "reforms" include for-profit educational management companies, charters, vouchers, scholarship tax credit neo-vouchers, reducing teacher staffs while expanding computer instruction, and also aggressively busting teachers' unions, emphasizing standardized testing and standardization of curriculum, replacing teacher seniority pay with pay for test scores, and putting in place restrictions on collective bargaining. These initiatives cut public spending on public education while transferring the financial burden to individuals. Those with more financial resources have greater choices. They cut spending by seeking both to decrease teacher pay and to increase "high stakes" forms of accountability that demand more test-based performance and hours of work. Such initiatives are creating the conditions for drastically higher teacher turnover, teacher burnout, and fewer experienced teachers[46] while expanding positivist, anti-intellectual, and anticritical forms of curriculum and pedagogy.

U.S. teachers receive preparation and certification mostly through state-certified university programs. Efforts to undermine teacher education programs in universities aim to shift control and ownership of teacher preparation out of public and not-for-profit academic centers of scholarship and into a for-profit marketplace defined through vocationalism and narrow service delivery. The teacher education profiteers are sharing the same script as the neoliberal assailants of K–12. The first move is to presume that teacher education is not a public good but rather a private service that should be framed and understood through the language of business with terms such as monopoly, choice, competition, and failure. The second move is to declare teacher education as "failed." In order to do so the usual cast of neoliberal policy wonks who have been calling for the privatization or end of public education (Chester Finn, Frederick Hess, Erik Hanushek, Paul T. Hill, Bruno Manno, Joseph Viteritti, Michelle Rhee, Michael Barber, E. D. Hirsh, and so on) have tirelessly called in mass media, written and distributed policy briefs, and built up government relationships in order to radically reevaluate the very value of teacher education. They promote several projects, including pushing alternative certification cleansed of theory, weakening the power of state boards of education, and pushing for privatization through think tanks and venture philanthropies. Such projects include the creation of "evaluation" organizations such as, most notoriously and influentially, the National Council on Teacher Quality (NCTQ), which counts several of these neoliberal policies' wonks among its advisory board members.

NCTQ targets teacher education programs for evaluation, using spurious methods such as evaluating course syllabi and treating a lack of data as negative evidence for program quality. *U.S. News and World Report*, a highly influential higher education ranking publication, is using NCTQ for its rankings of teacher education programs, despite the fact that NCTQ has completely different ways of evaluating programs from the rest of the *U.S. News* evaluation methods. NCTQ has a mafia-esque style of evaluating in which nonparticipating programs are warned that if they do not give demanded materials they will be evaluated anyway with a failing grade.[47] A number of scholars and professional associations, such as the American Association of Colleges of Teacher Education and groups of deans, have sharply criticized what they have widely termed "input-oriented" approaches to gathering data. NCTQ frames its evaluations as providing "consumers" of teacher education services with information for consumer choices in the teacher education market. The purpose, however, is to declare programs as failed and in need of market-based competition from the private sector.[48]

Redistributing control and governance over teacher education from universities and states to the private sector has a number of implications, including placing limits on what can and will be taught by teacher education programs. The parallel with corporate media is instructive here. For-profit media companies do not include critical content that challenges the institutional interests of the company. For example, corporate news programs do not report on or frame issues in ways that could undermine the financial interests of those organizations such as by reporting on media regulation legislation or providing alternative views on politics and economics from a narrow range of ideological assumptions.[49] Public and independent institutions that are not beholden to profit allow a greater range of ideological questioning and self and social critique. The implications for teacher education are significant as privatized teacher education programs will have institutional interests that run counter to the kinds of pedagogical approaches and curricula that encourage future teachers to understand the political, ethical, and historical power struggles that constitute the social fabric, that inform and frame knowledge, and that help teacher candidates to theorize their clinical experiences and future work in K–12 classrooms. Fostering teachers to become what Giroux has described as transformative intellectuals demands forms of teacher education that are socially engaged, political, and theoretical.[50] It is precisely these critical aspects of teacher education that are under attack in the neoliberal movement.

This is particularly evident in alternative certification programs that are in vogue and are being expanded in urban districts under the moniker "urban academies,"[51] which are funded and supported to a high degree by the venture philanthropists.[52] The venture philanthropies are promoting teacher education that merges methods with so-called content knowledge—allegedly neutral disciplinary subject matter. The crucial move here is in eliminating pedagogy and theory and treating knowledge as a neutral "deliverable." There is a high degree of convergence between the neoliberal tendency to emphasize numerically quantifiable measures of learning and the neoconservative tendency (typified by E. D. Hirsh, Diane Ravitch, and William Bennett) to promote a common core, culturally conservative curriculum deemed to be universally valuable and politically neutral.[53]

Anticritical K–12 Pedagogies Transform the Student Body and Work of Higher Education

The graduates of teacher education programs become the K–12 teachers of the students who will eventually become enrolled in colleges and universities. The anticritical tendencies of neoliberal teacher education instill future teachers with a number of values, assumptions, and dispositions that run counter to the best aspects of the critical tradition. The neoliberal perspective eschews the connection between knowledge and the broader social conditions informing its making, elides the formation of the self by social forces and the ways that such a process plays into acts of interpretation, and eliminates the ethical and political dimensions of teaching and learning. Perhaps one of the most significant anticritical tendencies is the positioning of the future teacher's relationship to knowledge. For example, test-based, numerically quantifiable, and decontextualized forms of knowledge are elevated over other forms of knowledge. High-stakes standardized tests put in place a simple equivalence between numerical test outcomes and future earning potential of students. *Professional* in the neoliberal discourse is being redefined to refer not to teachers who attend additional graduate school to expand their understanding of their subjects and to theorize and comprehend more deeply their practices in the classroom, but, increasingly, to learn pat methods that might increase student test scores regardless of the implications of teaching for standardized tests.[54]

Anticritical forms of teacher education participate in producing students who come to higher education wholly unprepared to engage with the kinds of questions and concerns that scholars at the heights of their fields study. In fact, higher education ought to be the model for K–12 forms of learning. How do scholars in higher education learn? Nobody shows up at the professor's door with a standardized test. The scholar is engaged in an academic community and is in dialogue with other scholars in the field verbally, in writing, and through the process of review. Yet rather than increasing the expectations for K–12 schooling by expanding its dialogic dimensions, teacher education and higher education is more often being subject to test-oriented demands for "accountability" that have been imposed on K–12 schooling. The same proponents of eroding the conditions of teacher work are demanding higher "performance" from teachers in terms of test scores. This is preposterous on a number of levels. First, the tests to a high degree measure cultural capital and affirm and reward or punish and denigrate the class position of the student. Second, of course, the question of who enrolls in teacher education programs has a lot to do with both the financial disincentives for teaching that include low pay and, now, job insecurity (through attacks on tenure and pay for experience and advanced education) and the punitive, disrespectful culture that has been forged toward teachers. Demands for numerical test-based "accountability" are crucially part of a project to erode teacher intellectual autonomy, decimate teacher work conditions, and create a system of high teacher turnover to burn out new teachers while suppressing labor costs. This is a recipe not only for transforming teaching from a profession into low-skill piece work but also for guaranteeing a workforce of inexperienced teachers.

Both higher education and K–12 education increasingly are subject to the call for schooling to be primarily economically useful. Attacks on the humanities, social sciences, and the arts and the call for funding only science, mathematics, and engineering education in Europe through Bologna and the right-wing British government parallel the trends in the United States for "investing" only in STEM (science, technology, engineering, mathematics) and for creating work-themed charters and public schools. According to the U.S. National Research Council and the National Science Foundation, high performance in the STEM fields tends to be a sign of a technologically advanced society and also indicates the fields necessary to supposedly sustain such a society. Such a prioritizing of science over the humanities and social sciences fails to address how the current model of capitalist growth tends toward ecological collapse, the proliferation and expansion of vast human inequalities and violence, and the failure to address human and ecological needs. Human-made crises, including global warming, and their current and anticipated devastating social effects cannot be dealt with primarily through the development of new technologies. These are not technical problems; they are human problems that have to do with human values and priorities, ways of life, and practices. For example, continuing to accept an economy structured around unlimited growth and individual commodity accumulation can only expand human and ecologically destructive patterns such as fossil fuel usage, global warming, and vast waste production.[55] By discounting the very traditions that offer the tools for addressing these social problems, such a framing of education undermines progress.

As Slovoj Zizek suggests, the possibility to not simply answer questions but to reformulate problems is a crucial task of critical thought and one that has socially useful and socially reconstructive and radical purposes.[56] The defunding of the humanities and social sciences on the basis of funding only "useful" disciplines represents an attack on those studies that have public purposes and ones that promise the distinctly useful possibility of revaluing social values.

The push to privatize teacher education typified by NCTQ, the right-wing think tanks, and the Department of Education under the Obama administration centrally involves elevating practical experience in classrooms while denigrating educational theory. There is a long tradition in education of claiming that experience speaks for itself, that understanding of educational approaches and practices can only be gained by being "in the trenches."[57] Critical pedagogy contends that experience never speaks for itself but rather always needs to be interpreted. Interpretation demands theory that can help one make sense of what one brings to the process of interpretation.

The neoliberal attack on teacher education seeks to remove courses in social and cultural foundations that are centrally concerned with offering students the tools to theorize their experiences in the classroom in relation to the broader society. This curricular transformation is being done by expanding the amount of time candidates spend in the classroom and by eliminating course work in the social and cultural foundations from privatized programs. Take, for example, a Chicago for-profit teacher education business called the American College of Education (ACE). For-profit education entrepreneur Randy Best (Voyager Expanded Learning Inc.) established ACE by purchasing DePaul University's suburban Barat campus in order to get Higher Learning Commission accreditation despite the accreditation being used to create new strictly online courses and programs with no relationship to either the DePaul College of Education or to Barat's prior history of being a teacher college. ACE cut a deal with the Chicago Public Schools under the leadership of Arne Duncan to merge online instruction with entirely clinical in-person "instruction." The masters programs in curriculum and instruction and educational leadership eliminate all traditional university course work as well as all social and cultural foundations courses. The Higher Learning Commission website lists ACE enrollment at 3,183 students, with the most recent year graduating 776 masters degrees. The reduced course load achieved by eliminating foundations courses, the use of part-time online-only faculty, and the elimination of university classrooms of course translates into greater profits for the owners of ACE. As a for-profit, the institution can withdraw these profits from the educational process rather than being obligated to reinvest any surplus.

During his tenure in the U.S. Department of Education, Arne Duncan has repeatedly called for expanding alternative certification—despite a lack of evidence for its success or effectiveness—has repeatedly criticized teacher education, and has called for education to be less theoretical and more practical. These rallies against theory and in favor of practicalism represent a resurgent positivism (radical empiricism that separates facts from the values that undergird and organize them) merged with an elevation of practice as tied to education-for-work.

These anti-intellectual reforms, including value-added assessment, the assault on teacher education, union-busting, and privatizations, are essentially prohibitions on thinking; indeed, they are utterly antithetical to teachers acting as intellectuals or performing the public role of fostering that dialogue, debate, and critical thought that is the lifeblood of public democratic life outside of schools. As the public problems facing humanity—from nuclear Armageddon to eco-collapse to technological disasters—appear to most citizens to be reaching a threatening point of no return, public schooling is one of the last public spheres not yet thoroughly overrun by commercial culture. It should be one point of hope where youth, the very embodiment of hope for the future, can be invested with the tools and skills for creative and deep thought to comprehend and ruthlessly criticize the present so as to imagine a future that is not just free and equal, prosperous and peaceful, but survivable.

Behind corporate school reforms such as charters, vouchers, value-added assessment, urban "portfolio districts," and commercialism there are some myths that need to be named and challenged. One is that public education has "failed" (a convenient market metaphor) and that it is now time to "give the market a chance." The reality is that the gross inequalities in public education are the result of the linkage of real estate markets to school funding and the long-standing influence of business in thoroughly shaping the select school failures of today—from the Business Roundtable to the National Association of Manufacturers, from corporate philanthropies to direct business partnerships. The current state of schools owes much to the long-standing mistake of having given the market a chance.[58]

A related myth is that when privatization advocates declare public schooling "a failure" (as has Bill Gates and a panoply of CEOs and pro-privatization policy wonks) they do not mean *all* public schools have failed. They are really uttering a racially coded attack on working-class and poor people who have been historically denied fair distribution of educational resources. Now the same predominantly white beneficiaries of unequal distribution of educational resources are participating in profiteering by targeting working-class and poor students of color, schools, and communities for privatization. Why have the educational profiteers failed to make inroads into the rich white suburbs of major cities? These schools and communities have been the beneficiaries of the constitutive struggle over public space and public resources and have no interest in having their public dollars skimmed off for the owners and managers, lawyers, and investors in EdisonLearning, KIPP (Knowledge Is Power Program), and so on. This leads to one more seldom recognized reality.

The kind of schooling pushed by the privatization advocates aims to transform a current dual system of public schooling into another dual system of public schooling. In the current dual system, elite public schools in rich, predominantly white communities prepare managers, leaders, and professionals for the top of the economy and the state while the underfunded public schools in poor, working-class, and predominantly nonwhite communities prepare the docile, disciplined workforce for the bad jobs at the bottom of the economy and for exclusion from the economy altogether. Despite the ceaseless neoliberal and liberal rhetoric of crisis and failure, the public schools (as Freire, Bourdieu, Ollman, and others recognize) do exactly what they are supposed to do: they produce a stratified workforce while sanctifying inequality as a matter of individual merit or talent. The neoliberal privatization reforms maintain the dual system, leaving in place the elite public schools but targeting poor schools and predominantly students of color to turn them into *short-term* profit opportunities in numerous ways: the contracting, testing, and tutoring schemes but also for-profit management and all the ancillary profits that can be generated through privatization—including the public funds that will pour into marketing charter schools to prospective "customers" through advertising and public relations, and the lucrative real estate deals needed to establish charter schools. At present, the lower end of the dual system provides a *deferred* investment in low-pay, low-skill disciplined workers and fodder for the for-profit prison industry and the military.

Privatization targets the low end of the dual system and pillages the public sector for short-term profits, benefitting mostly the ruling class and professional class ("poverty pimping") while doing nothing to transform the dual system of public education into a single system as good as its best parts throughout. For investors in privatization, the benefits are double: money can be made in the short run by draining public tax revenue, while the future exploitable workforce can still be produced for the long run. And as the investors are benefitting twice, they can feel good that they are giving poor students "every opportunity" to benefit themselves. Of course, class mobility is declining, unemployment is rising, and economic inequality and exclusion is shifting onto school kids who will need to be, in the words of Thomas Friedman, more entrepreneurial to get and keep scarcer jobs.[59] Such school reform ideology displaces the violence of the capitalist economy onto the weakest and most vulnerable citizens: children. As I write, one in five U.S. children is on food stamps, with ballooning rates of child homelessness, while inequalities in wealth have reached greater proportions than in the Gilded Age.[60] The crucial point is that the goal should not be to emulate the financial bailout and see how we can all help to subsidize the rich getting richer by replicating a more lucrative system of dual education—the rich part still public and the poor part privatized. The goal must be ending the dual education system.

The first step involves following the rest of the industrialized nations and federalizing the educational funding system. The second step involves funding the schools and students in need more than the students in the best schools currently receive in order to compensate for the additional obstacles faced by poverty (objections to this should reckon with the fact that a single soldier in Afghanistan as of 2011 costs the public $1.2 million per year[61]). The third step involves revaluing teaching as the most important profession by treating it as an intellectual, socially transformative pursuit rather than a technical skill. The fourth step involves replacing the pedagogical and evaluative system of high-stakes standardized testing with one modeled on the processes of learning at the heights of knowledge, the university, and making the teaching profession a genuinely academic one (not just a professional one, as liberals argue, and not one that replicates the corporate workforce, as neoliberals and corporate reformers argue). The fifth step requires recognizing that the culture inside schools is inseparable from the culture outside of schools, meaning that a public and democratic rationale for public schooling has to be linked to a collective goal of expanding democratic social relations. As such, systemic school improvement has to begin to take seriously how schooling is involved in subject formation and how it either affirms or contests relations of power and domination in the broader society.

CHAPTER TWO

THE FAILURE OF EVIDENCE IN CORPORATE SCHOOL POLICY IMPLEMENTATION

THE CASE OF THE URBAN PORTFOLIO DISTRICT

Introduction: The Failure of Evidence in Corporate School Reform

This chapter reveals the extent to which recent corporate school reforms are being spearheaded and implemented despite a lack of evidence for their success and despite numerous glaring problems for the most part recognized by advocates. While this chapter focuses on urban portfolio districts, it makes a much larger point about a number of corporate school reforms. Urban portfolio district reform is composed of numerous other corporate reforms. As the chapter makes clear, these reforms—such as chartering, management contracting, turnarounds, and high-stakes-test–based closures—are being implemented by policy experts without evidence for effectiveness, not even evidence on their own terms: tests and costs. Whereas the previous chapter offers a more comprehensive explanation based on ideology and material interest for this phenomenon, this chapter details the lack of evidence behind the claims of the reformers and discusses a number of reasons for implementation even without evidence in the social science research that they work. A version of this chapter originally appeared as a policy brief with the National Education Policy Center.

In the latter half of the past decade, school districts in several large cities, including New York, Chicago, Washington, D.C., and post-Katrina New Orleans, began to implement a new model of urban school decentralization often called *portfolio districts*. Other school districts, including those in Denver and Cleveland, are following suit in what appears to be a growing trend. The portfolio strategy has become increasingly prominent in educational policy circles, think-tank and philanthropy literature, and education news reporting. U.S. Secretary of Education Arne Duncan embraced and implemented the portfolio model as "CEO" of Chicago Public Schools in the form of Renaissance 2010 and continues to promote its elements in such national policy as Race to the Top and in proposed revisions to the No Child Left Behind legislation. The premise supporting portfolio districts is that if education vendors compete on the basis of proposed innovations, with a school superintendent monitoring activities, children will receive greater opportunity for academic success. This chapter examines the available evidence for the viability of this premise and the proposals (for example, making all schools in a district charter schools) that flow from it.

A number of urban districts have embraced or are considering adopting the portfolio model. National policy also favors the idea. However, there have been no substantive studies of the portfolio district approach.[1] The only relevant research to date has been on its constituent elements, which include (1) decentralization, (2) charter school expansion, (3) reconstituting/closing "failing" schools, and (4) test-based accountability.[2] As will be detailed in the following pages, the available scholarly peer-reviewed evidence on these various constituent elements shows no effect or negative effects on student achievement and on educational costs.

Some readers may be surprised to learn that there is a scarcity of research on portfolio districts or such constituent elements as closures because there is an abundance of policy literature, published especially by think tanks. However, the published policy literature advocating implementation of the portfolio model and its elements most often makes assertions without providing credible evidence for its claims. For example, all of the six relevant articles available from the scholarly database Academic Search Premiere give favorable reports on the portfolio model, but none of them either constitutes or references careful empirical study reviewed by a community of policy scholars.[3] Much of such advocacy writing published about the portfolio model and its constituent elements is generated by authors housed in or connected to policy think tanks, which tend to have political and policy agendas. Lacking to date are studies by independent scholars who are concerned with accurate information rather than with a result supporting a preconceived policy agenda.[4] In terms of advocacy publications, a single market-oriented think tank, the Center on Reinventing Public Education (CRPE), seems to have "cornered the market" on promoting the implementation of the portfolio model. While CRPE describes itself as conducting independent research, it generally advocates a number of market-oriented approaches to school reform (pay for performance, charters, choice), publishes the most outspoken advocates of imagining public schooling as a private consumable (Paul Hill, Jane Hannaway, Eric Hanushek), and shares researchers with the market-oriented think tank the Urban Institute.[5]

If we ask why the portfolio model has been implemented without the support of evidence, there are at least three possible answers: (1) advocacy literature is being accepted as evidence, (2) the constituent elements of the portfolio approach appear to add up to a reasonable model because they each appear to be supported by credible evidence, and (3) some advocates assume that evidence is not necessary because the public system has "failed" and now it is time to give radical experiments a chance. In the following chapter, I discuss a fourth explanation that is the creation of an entirely new strata of private market bureaucracy, which I term "the new market bureaucracy" and which represents a dramatic shift in governance from public to private sector under the guise of "de-bureaucratizing" the allegedly hopeless inefficient public sector. This shift in control over bureaucratic infrastructure coincides with shifts in ownership and control over culture, curriculum, and pedagogy in schools.

Early Forms of Decentralization: Administrative and Community Control

It is important to understand that the portfolio model differs radically from the district "decentralization" reforms of the 1980s. Writing in the journal *Urban Education* in 1991, P. Wohlstetter and K. McCurdy characterized the earlier decentralization trends as follows: "Cloaked in many terms—restructuring, school-based management, shared decision making—school decentralization shifts formal decision making from the central administration to a smaller decision-making arena—the school. Decentralized schools alter the educational power structure by empowering school personnel, community groups, or both to make decisions about budgets, personnel, and programs."[6]

In the early 1990s school decentralization generally took one of two forms. One was administrative decentralization, which moved the power to make some decisions from a district's central administration to smaller units within the district. In this form, decision-making authority moved downward while accountability remained at the top with the central administration and the board of education. A typical example was school-based management (SBM)/shared decision making (SDM), implemented in Miami in 1987–1988. SDM involved "allow[ing] teachers and principals to develop their own system for the total management of their individual schools, with minimum direction from higher authority."[7]

A second form of decentralization, community control, shifted both decision-making and accountability for outcomes to the local community, including citizens and other noneducation specialists. One example occurred in Chicago in 1988, after Chicago was singled out as the worst urban school district in the nation by then Secretary of Education William Bennett and after an unusual coalition of business people and parents lobbied the state legislature for dramatic change. This community-controlled decentralization was implemented with mixed results.[8]

In both administrative and community control versions of decentralization, teachers, local administrators, and teachers' unions had varying degrees of decision-making authority, with community control adding community representatives to the mix. Administrative control is approached differently in the portfolio model.

The New Decentralization: Portfolio Districts

As in the case of administrative decentralization, portfolio districts shift administrative decision making to local educational units while central administration retains accountability for educational outcomes. A significant difference is that the portfolio approach shifts control downward—not to schools or units of schools administered collaboratively by local administrators, teachers, communities, and unions, but instead by largely moving control to private educational contractors. These include for-profit and nonprofit charter school operators, educational management organizations, and charter management organizations.[9]

Administrative and community-control decentralization peaked in popularity in the late 1980s, by which time fourteen states had adopted some form of
decentralization. By the early to mid-1990s, disenchantment with the approach
had begun to set in, and the push for state takeover of failing districts or placing those districts under direct mayoral control began.[10] The portfolio model
combines an emphasis on highly concentrated control at the top of the district
(by superintendents, mayors, and state agencies) with downward delegation to
contractors who are expected to demonstrate high performance in return for
relative autonomy (less community accountability). The four large urban districts
that have implemented the portfolio model have district heads who report either
to a mayor who has taken control of the district or, in the case of New Orleans,
to a state that has seized control of the district from the city. The top-down
retention of administrative control is far more extensive than in older forms of
decentralization, and the downward delegation of administrative control goes
to different parties—that is, to contractors.[11]

This portfolio approach draws on the metaphor of stock investment. The
district superintendent is imagined as a stock investor who has a portfolio of
investments (schools). The superintendent creates a portfolio of contractors and
subsequently holds the investments that "perform" (in terms of student achievement) and ends the contracts (or sells) those investments that "don't perform."
The approach merges four radical corporate restructuring ideas:[12] (1) decentralization, (2) charter school expansion, (3) school closures with charter replacements, and (4) accountability, largely through testing.[13] The portfolio district is
imagined as a circuit of continuous improvement in which schools are assessed
based on test scores. If scores are low, schools are subject to possible closure (or
mass firings) and to being reopened as charters. If the charters subsequently fail
to show desired improvements, they in turn are subject to possible closure and
replacement by still other contractors. The portfolio district concept puts into
place what has been increasingly discussed in educational policy literature as
market-based "creative destruction" or "churn."[14]

This perspective considers public schools to be comparable to private enterprise, with competition a key element to success. Like businesses that cannot turn
sufficient profit, schools that cannot produce test scores higher than competitors'
must be "allowed" to "go out of business." This metaphor persists in education
policy despite frequent observations that the correspondence between enterprise
and education is highly questionable at best. It presumes public schools have the
same mission as business, generating profit, when public schools exist to serve the

public interest. It assumes markets to be competitive rather than monopolistic, and it presumes government regulation to be at odds with markets. In reality, certain industries (entertainment, defense, telecommunications, transportation, agriculture, for example) are monopolistic with significant barriers to entry, while the private sector may rely on the public sector, government intervention, or both for survival (government subsidy and regulation of the financial and automotive industries to save them from collapse, for example). In addition, unlike industry, public education cannot control its "raw materials"—that is, its students. The bad metaphor also results in mistaken approaches to pedagogy and curriculum by treating knowledge as necessarily measurable in quantifiable ways and as a private deliverable. There is no place in this view to understand knowledge as dialogic, constructed, or critical (as discussed in Chapters 1 and 4). Despite these difficulties, the metaphor persists—and this reasoning drives the portfolio model.

Given the prominence of the portfolio model, it is important to understand what evidence supports the approach, especially in the two areas of particular interest in policy discussions, student achievement, and cost. The following review is based on a search of the Academic Search Premiere library database, incorporating all available sub-databases.[15]

Evidence and the Portfolio District Approach

While there is a large body of educational policy research on decentralization, nearly all of this research takes up earlier versions of decentralization that emphasize either local administrative or community control. There have been no peer-reviewed scholarly studies of the portfolio model. Nor have there been non-peer-reviewed empirical studies of it. Instead, available literature offers suggestions and strategies for implementation as well as arguments for the approach and cautions about potential pitfalls.

Although studies of earlier approaches to decentralizing school districts do exist, they offer little help in comprehending the potential effects of portfolio districts because the delegation of power to contractors differs so strikingly from earlier delegation to school personnel, organizations, and communities. Much more relevant to evaluation of the portfolio model might be existing studies of the effects of public school privatization through contracting with for-profit or nonprofit providers. However, these studies would not account for other elements of portfolio district approach and their impact on such contracting. That is, the portfolio approach merges contracting with several other major reform strategies, including charter school expansion, school closures with charter replacements, and test-based accountability. Because these diverse strands are so intertwined in portfolio districts, earlier studies that focused primarily on the shift of authority can offer little or no information about whether the approach will do what its proponents hope: raise student achievement scores, decrease costs, or both.

In theory, it might be possible to evaluate elements of the portfolio district model in isolation and then speculate as to their combined effects. However, this prospect is problematic because each element will likely affect the others, rendering individual assessment of each element difficult or impossible. For example, the strategy of charter school development has been studied independently. The research shows that charter school development yields mixed to slightly negative effects on "student achievement."[16] However, when charters are implemented in a mix of strategies that might include school closures, mass firings, test-based assessment, and possibly special funding, it becomes virtually impossible to measure the alleged effectiveness of the charter component independently. The portfolio district created in New Orleans after Hurricane Katrina is a case in point.[17]

When the New Orleans public schools were closed and networks of charter schools subsequently opened there, a large number of students had been displaced by the storm. In addition, a large sum of money was put into the charter schools created in the new Recovery School District (RSD). Much of that money came from large philanthropic organizations, such as the Bill and Melinda Gates Foundation and the Broad Foundation. Assessing the test-based effectiveness of the RSD charters relative to the schools they replaced would require accounting for the displacement of students due to the storm, accounting for the resulting racial and class demographic shifts, and accounting for the infusion of money into the RSD charters by grant givers and government.

A more meaningful interpretation would also need to take into account the history of public disinvestment in the district and professional-class white flight that resulted in the worst-funded public school district in the nation prior to the storm. An even more meaningful evaluation of quality would raise the less quantifiable questions as to the extent to which teaching in those schools fostered in students the knowledge, skills, and dispositions necessary to interpret and respond to their experiences of the events in relation to the broader social forces informing those experiences.[18] Claims about improvements yielded by RSD charters are hotly contested and as yet unsubstantiated by peer-reviewed research.

Paul Vallas, who heads the RSD, and Paul Pastorek, the state superintendent, laud student achievement gains in RSD schools and are expanding the RSD through-out Louisiana by requiring principals to sign memorandums of understanding that their schools are subject to test-based accountability and potential closure, chartering, or other restructuring. However, Thomas Robichaux of the Orleans Parish School Board contends that while achievement scores in the RSD schools have risen, RSD gains have lagged relative to the Orleans Parish schools, despite the fact that RSD schools enjoy roughly twice the per-pupil infusion of money.[19]

The difficulties of assessing the impact of individual elements of the port-folio district approach suggest that the best and possibly the only way to know whether the strategy achieves its aims is to evaluate it as a whole. As will be discussed, even the most outspoken proponents of the portfolio approach offer the post-Katrina New Orleans example as a demonstration of how difficult it is to measure achievement gains in the portfolio approach. As has been noted, while no peer-reviewed studies of the portfolio district approach in its entirety have appeared, a search of relevant literature did yield six articles on the topic.[20] None of these, however, sheds any light on the question of whether improve-ments in achievement or cost have been realized. The lack of evidence has not deterred proponents from issuing reports and arguments offering both promises and warnings. Most of these publications are very brief (a single paragraph to three pages) promotions for the portfolio idea, unsupported by evidence.

Unique to the literature, but also unsupported by peer-reviewed scholarly empirical evidence, is an October 2009 report issued by the Center on Reinvent-ing Public Education (CRPE) at the University of Washington, whose advocacy efforts were mentioned earlier. The publication, titled *Portfolio School Districts for Big Cities: An Interim Report*, advocates portfolio district development and implementation: "To telegraph this report's message: the portfolio idea has great promise, but making it work requires a great deal of time, money, and political capital applied over many years. No locality is likely to benefit by adopting it temporarily as a 'flavor of the month' or by cherry picking some parts of it and leaving other parts unimplemented."[21] However, the report informs readers that "it is too soon to make a bottom-line assessment of the effects of the portfolio idea on student achievement, but [this report] suggests how such an assessment can (and in what ways it should not) be done."[22] This interim report was to be followed in 2011 by a fuller report on performance, but the interim report warns that it is likely to be impossible in the future to evaluate whether the portfolio district approach has been successful:

It is unlikely, however, that we can ever give a simple answer to the question, "Have the cities that adopted a portfolio strategy benefited from it?" This is so for several reasons, including that districts started in different places and moved at different paces toward full implementation.... Everyone will want to judge the portfolio approach according to whether students learned more or less than before. But this will be easier said than done. Crude juxtapositions—like comparing city students' average gains to average gains statewide—leave too many differentiating factors (e.g., immigration, transiency, family disruptions) uncontrolled.[23]

Thus, the report promotes the portfolio district strategy even as it acknowledges it may be impossible ever to demonstrate clear benefits from it.

CRPE's interim report also notes the difficulty of assessing individual components of the portfolio as an indirect measurement of its overall potential: "A piecemeal approach—for example, calculating gain scores for students who attended new schools and comparing them to gains in the rest of the district—could easily produce misleading results."[24] In addition, CRPE warns against overly optimistic expectations: "Though new schools are at the core of a portfolio strategy, success in every case should not be expected. There is a risk of failure in creating new schools, even if they imitate existing successful schools. Nor is it clear how long it should take for new schools to reach their full potential with respect to student performance."[25]

Thus CRPE, the staunchest advocate for portfolio districts, offers several cautions about the portfolio strategy—including some about measuring achievement, making it difficult to understand the rationale for its undaunted support of the approach. On the one hand, the report clearly states that CRPE considers student achievement the most important measure of improvement:

Thus, the bottom-line question is whether districtwide gain scores have improved continuously over time, not only for students on average but also for poor and minority students formerly assigned to schools with very average gains. These questions could be answered districtwide, for different levels of schooling, or for different demographic groups.[26]

On the other hand, in the very next sentence the report acknowledges that this is "a very difficult analysis, given the need to follow large numbers of students over several years, and to take full account of changes in neighborhood and school demographic competition." Even more surprising than this observation that it is doubtful whether the stipulated criteria for success can be reliably measured is the observation that no reliable empirical evidence exists to support the strategy nonetheless being promoted: "Despite the claims of proponents and critics alike, no existing study can be considered definitive because none has used this form of analysis."[27] The CRPE report goes on to propose other ways to assess the value and success of the portfolio approach, including "observing changes in the schools available, their distribution among neighborhoods, ability of poor and minority children to get into their first choices of schools, teacher turnover and the numbers of teachers applying for jobs in schools serving low-income and minority neighborhoods, etc."[28] Thus, having stated that the measure of success must be achievement gains, the report notes that no definitive evidence exists to support the expectation of gains and that no way to measure gains attributable to the portfolio approach is on the horizon. Despite this apparently significant difficulty, CRPE persists in its advocacy, simply suggesting a menu of indirect measures of portfolio success.

Although no comprehensive scholarly study of the portfolio district approach has been undertaken, some partial assessments of student achievement and costs have been made in two of the four large urban districts implementing the strategy. In Chicago, the *Tribune* analyzed state student test data for Renaissance 2010 schools and found that "scores from the elementary schools created under Renaissance 2010 are nearly identical to the city average, and scores at the remade high schools are below the already abysmal city average."[29] The article continues with other concerns about Chicago's portfolio approach. "The moribund test scores follow other less than enthusiastic findings about Renaissance 2010—that displaced students ended up mostly in other low-performing schools and that mass closings led to youth violence as rival gang members ended up in the same classrooms. Together, they suggest the initiative hasn't lived up to its promise by this, its target year."[30]

Three other partial studies of Renaissance 2010 have appeared. One was funded by the Renaissance Schools Fund (RSF), the funding arm of Renaissance 2010, which has raised $50 million to spend on the portfolio approach.[31] Thus far RSF has awarded $30 million to sixty-three new schools. The RSF-funded report conducted by SRI found that "children in the fund-supported schools had low academic performance and posted test score gains identical to students in nearby neighborhood schools."[32] This evaluation does not account for other effects of the school closure dimension of the portfolio approach. The Chicago Consortium on School Research at the University of Chicago studied the effects of the Renaissance 2010 closures, finding that "students from closed schools landed, for the most part, at campuses that were just as bad and then progressed at the same predictably low levels."[33] It also found that students from closed schools who then attended higher-performing schools experienced a positive impact in terms of academic progress—but these were in the minority.

Despite inconclusive or negative results, Ron Huberman, the successor CEO to Arne Duncan in Chicago, made clear that he would expand the initiative. Renaissance 2010 was initiated by the Civic Committee of the Commercial Club of Chicago (a century-old organization representing Chicago corporations), which commissioned corporate consultant A.T. Kearney to write the school plan. Mayor Daley, who had control over Chicago Public Schools, championed the approach as well, framing the discussion in such familiar metaphorical market terms as "competition," "choice," and public-private partnerships. Although Huberman's administration never issued a study, he "said he has crunched the numbers and about one-third of the new schools are outperforming their neighborhood counterparts; one-third are identical in performance; the rest do worse."[34] The difficulties of evaluating the portfolio approach in Chicago is heightened by the ways that school closures were done, with closings based not only on alleged test scores but also on claims about building underutilization. Critics of the school closures have alleged uneven criteria for assessing performance and have suggested that the pattern of school closures and chartering aligned with urban gentrification plans.

In New Orleans's RSD, partial evidence is even less clear than in Chicago. Six scholarly peer-reviewed articles had appeared as of March 5, 2010, but none included achievement data or cost data. As has been noted, student achievement outcomes and relative costs are vigorously debated. Defenders of the RSD point to the Stanford CREDO study[35] of charters nationwide, which shows charters faring on par to worse than traditional public schools in student achievement, but which showed Louisiana charters faring better than traditional public schools. Critics of the study have questioned its methodology and selective use of data as well as the potential effects of unequal financial investments in charter versus noncharter schools.[36]

CRPE's interim report also addressed costs of portfolio implementation. It reported that the four large urban districts continued to pay for "salaries, other instructional costs, and facilities rent and maintenance" while philanthropy provided funds for innovation.[37] The amounts and uses of philanthropic funds differed in the districts, with some supporting charter management organizations, some supporting test-based database tracking projects, some funding an effort to encourage teachers to give up tenure for higher salaries or pay for performance, and some funding the creation of an independent research institution.

Though the exact amounts of money spent on portfolio district initiatives are not known, CRPE estimates that

> The amounts available have been significant, by some accounts as high as $200 million in New York City, half that amount in Chicago, and over $50 million in New Orleans. Philanthropic contributions to D.C. have been smaller to date, in part because the district has barely started to build external support organizations and in part because foundations are waiting to fulfill their pledges to the new teacher salary scheme.[38]

This dependence upon philanthropic funding for innovation generates uncertainty about future costs and future financing in portfolio districts. CRPE hopes that a future report will be able to answer this critical question: "Can the new support organizations, once established, operate on fees received from schools and the district, or will they require continued foundation funding?"[39]

This question about future funding raises other as yet unanswered questions about whether philanthropic foundations will have the resources and the will to continue portfolio funding, whether districts will have the resources and the will to replace any withdrawn foundation funding (economic changes result in sometimes vast changes in foundation wealth and capacity to continue funding, while revamped priorities by boards and directors can mean decisions to end funding of particular projects), or whether some as yet unidentified source of funding will be found to cover any future gap in public school budgets. Other complexities regarding foundation financing involve the use of private foundation funds to "leverage" public spending in directions that may be at odds with the public will and public interest. In particular, the large "venture philanthropies"—the Gates, Broad, and Walton foundations—have been successful at using publicly subsidized foundation wealth strategically to influence elements of privatization-oriented portfolio reform, including charter school expansion, vouchers, "neovouchers" (publicly funded tax credits for private tuition), linkage of teacher pay to test-based achievement, and school turnaround and closure efforts.[40]

Evidence and Constituent Elements of Portfolio District Approach

The proponents of the portfolio district approach at the Center on Reinventing Public Education make a strong case that the complexity of the portfolio approach makes it difficult to evaluate, and that it should not be evaluated or implemented piecemeal. Yet, legislators, administrators, and other decision makers may be tempted to ignore such cautions if there were evidence that one or several elements of the approach had demonstrated effectiveness. It may therefore be useful to demonstrate that even if it were reasonable to evaluate the approach in terms of the promise of its constituent elements, there still is no evidence available to support its implementation.

As has been noted, studies of earlier decentralization efforts are of little value because the portfolio model differs radically from earlier approaches. A meaningful study would need to focus on how shifting control to boards of contractors affected student achievement and administrative cost, but no evidence exists on this topic. Also lacking is evidence on the effects of contracting when merged with more concentrated superintendent control under mayoral or state takeover. Therefore, the only constituent elements of the portfolio approach that have been rigorously studied are charter schools, school closures and turnarounds, and test-based accountability.

Studies of charter school effects on achievement show mixed to negative results in comparison to traditional public schools, and they offer no information on comparative costs.[41] Of ninety-three peer-reviewed scholarly articles available on school closures, none offers empirical evidence regarding their effects on student achievement or cost; five available peer-reviewed studies of turnarounds also offer no information on these criteria. The impact of test-based accountability can be evaluated based on the successes or failures of No Child Left Behind. Between 2008 and 2010, fifty-three peer-reviewed articles available in full text form were published on No Child Left Behind and the key words "student achievement."[42] Of the fifty-three, the vast majority raised methodological, theoretical, and practical problems with this experiment in test-based accountability. None frame NCLB as demonstrating the effectiveness of test-based accountability, although some do retain hope for the concept. Available evidence suggests, however, that on the whole NCLB has failed to raise student achievement or to close the racial "achievement gap."[43] The literature also reflects concerns about cost because federal funding allocated was insufficient to fund the testing agenda—and even the insufficient amount promised was never fully provided.[44]

**Table 2.1 Summary of Scholarly Peer-Reviewed Evidence
Available on the Portfolio District Approach**

	Student Achievement	Cost
New York	Data unavailable	Data unavailable
Chicago	Data unavailable	Data unavailable
New Orleans	Data unavailable	Data unavailable
Washington, D.C.	Data unavailable	Data unavailable

Source: Academic Search Premiere, March 6, 2010.

**Table 2.2 Summary of Scholarly Peer-Reviewed Evidence Available
on Constituent Elements of Portfolio District Approach**

	Student Achievement	Cost
Portfolio Decentralization	Data unavailable	Data unavailable
Charter School Creation	Mixed to negative evidence	Data unavailable
School Closure	Data unavailable	Data unavailable
Test-Based Accountability	Negative evidence	Data unavailable
School Turnarounds	Data unavailable	Data unavailable
Teacher Pay for Test Performance	Data unavailable	Data unavailable

Source: Academic Search Premiere, March 6, 2010.

**Table 2.3 Evidence Available on Portfolio District
Approach Based In Proponents' Claims**

	Student Achievement	Cost in Addition to Regular District Funding
Portfolio Decentralization	Data unavailable	Data unavailable
Charter School Creation	Mixed to negative evidence	Data unavailable
School Closure	Data unavailable	Data unavailable
Test-Based Accountability	Negative evidence	Data unavailable
School Turnarounds	Data unavailable	Data unavailable
Teacher Pay for Test Performance	Data unavailable	Data unavailable

Source: Academic Search Premiere, March 6, 2010.

Lacking Evidence, the Lessons of Experience

As has been indicated, there is no empirical evidence to suggest that the portfolio approach will deliver the achievement gains that advocates like CRPE consider its "bottom-line" benefit. Proponents acknowledge that definitive measures of student achievement that can account for the complexity of the proposed radical changes do not exist. Rather than predicting that such analytic tools can and will be developed, CRPE encourages alternative, indirect means of measuring success. Moreover, it counsels patience in awaiting positive results: "Friends and enemies of the portfolio approach will seize on quick results, but their claims can serve political ends, not render balanced judgment of a complex and long-term strategy."[45]

Administrators and legislators ought to be aware of just how significant the problems with achievement measurement in portfolio districts are—as even advocates acknowledge. No evidence exists to suggest student achievement gains can be expected; no expectation exists for the development of analytic tools capable of measuring the portfolio approach's effect on achievement, its central promise. This situation presents administrators and legislators with the difficult task of justifying "reform" with no supporting achievement evidence and no foreseeable possibility of such evidence. Add to this unknown and currently unknowable information on student achievement, the clearer picture of high financial costs, effects of those high costs on other public expenditures, uncertainties for future funding, political fallout, and the potential adverse effect of the reform on other more promising educational reforms (reduced class size, for example, or comprehensive social support programs linked to educational reforms, as in the Harlem Children's Zone), and in sum, the portfolio district approach looks like a recipe for high risk and no clear reward. Experience to date offers reason to expect such negative complications.

Existing portfolio implementation has been expensive, and future financial support for it is uncertain. Large philanthropies such as the Gates and Broad foundations have provided substantive funding, understanding schooling as a "private consumable service" that "promotes business remedies, reforms, and assumptions."[46] Although educational philanthropy accounts for just a fraction of educational spending in the United States, its institutions have recently acquired disproportionate influence and control over educational policy and practice.[47] While such philanthropies provide seed money to promote what they term "reform," if the federal government were to encourage continuation of the seeded portfolio approaches, the impact on district funding could be enormous. Even the Center on Reinventing Public Education suggests that a problem with the portfolio approach is that philanthropic support can dry up. However, CRPE does not explore how such philanthropically supported initiatives as teacher bonus pay (Washington, D.C.), research institutes (New York City), or ancillary support for charter development, when suddenly defunded by the philanthropies, may require districts to choose between core operations expenditures and portfolio initiatives.[48] It is worth considering that districts might be forced to move limited resources away from such areas as teacher pay, physical site maintenance, and materials and into infrastructure for various portfolio initiatives. This scenario is especially likely because short-run federal stimulus money supporting teacher salaries from 2009 is running out even as states and districts face budget short-falls at levels not seen for decades.

Social and political strife also seem likely complications in portfolio districts, as has been seen in Chicago and New Orleans, and more recently in Providence, Rhode Island, following the radical mass firings of teachers in a "turnaround." Social conflict in Chicago made international news when neighborhood gang lines were disregarded in the closing and opening of schools under Renaissance 2010. This corporate-instituted portfolio plan in the mayor-controlled district resulted in Fenger High School opening with 100 percent new faculty and students imported from various closed neighborhood schools. As a result, the school's teachers, staff, and administrators lacked crucial knowledge of the community and the students to prevent a melee that resulted in the much publicized death of student Derrion Albert, widely watched on the web. George Schmidt of *Substance News* wrote,

> But more than most other gang induced murders in Chicago—and affecting the public schools—the murder of Derrion Albert is the result not only of the city's massive drug gang problem, but of the Chicago Board of Education's policies of "New Schools" and "School Turnaround." By closing Calumet, Engelwood, and Carver high schools—and forcing the most challenging students from those schools into Fenger and nearby schools—Mayor Daley and Chicago schools officials appointed by him guaranteed that Fenger would "fail." When Fenger failed, Daley's school board voted to fire all of Fenger's teachers and force a program called "turnaround" on Fenger. The destabilization resulted in chaos in September 2009.[49]

Such intentional instability (churn, creative destruction) is central to the portfolio model. Urban districts may benefit most, however, from thoughtful and planned efforts to create stability and to nurture social attachments in order to strengthen communities that are already destabilized by a historical legacy of disinvestment, racialized poverty, and violence. Geoffrey Canada's Harlem Children's Zone is, for example, a highly publicized example of a comprehensive, community-based development project that incorporates public support for development throughout the life span. Although Canada has become an unfortunate mouthpiece for those who seek to promote charters de-linked from comprehensive lifelong public services, his project and the federal Promise Neighborhoods initiative (both of which aim to implement prenatal through university comprehensive stable social supports) are good counter examples to the churn logic of portfolio districts. Unfortunately, rather than funding comprehensive lifelong public supports the Obama administration has largely underfunded them in favor of churn-oriented corporate school reforms like Race to the Top and NCLB organized around competition and choice. Such policies share the destabilizing logic of portfolio districts. In addition to lifelong public supports for communities, development projects ideally would also centrally feature a critical pedagogical component that would enable youth and adults to critically comprehend and transform the broader social, political, economic, and cultural forces that produce the oppression that they experience. It is not enough to link educational reform to a reinvigorated welfare state that leaves unquestioned existing relations of power.

In addition, and in direct contrast to earlier decentralization efforts that moved control into the hands of local school personnel, the portfolio model embeds as strategy mass firings and the exclusion of teachers, community members, and unions from local administrative processes. Associated complications include the effects of de-unionization on teacher work conditions, hiring of certified (and uncertified) teachers, and retention of experienced teachers. The practical effects of such significant and potentially disruptive changes in portfolio districts are unstudied, although difficulties of staffing poor schools with qualified teachers are already well known, as are the effects of these policies on their own.[50]

What Is Driving the Portfolio District Approach?

The closure of traditional public schools and the opening of charter schools are central elements of the portfolio district approach. Therefore, it may make sense to understand the portfolio strategy less as an initiative for decentralization and more as an initiative for privatization. In fact, advocates of the portfolio district strategy, including the Center on Reinventing Public Education, the venture philanthropies, and the Secretary of Education, support portfolio approaches because they put in place privatized choice schemes that allegedly introduce "market discipline" in the form of competition and choice.[51] Those considering the portfolio approach might consider the possibility that at least some of the enthusiasm for portfolio districts may be vested in their ability to promote a privatization agenda. Despite widespread enthusiasm for privatization, the scholarly evidence does not suggest that for-profit or nonprofit private schools outperform traditional public schools in terms of student achievement, as illustrated by Philadelphia's ambitious experiment with varied providers.[52]

To return to the portfolio approach on its own terms, the justification for it seems to rest on metaphorical business images that substitute for evidence. As has been discussed, a key portfolio metaphor casts the district head as a manager buying and selling investments (schools and contractors) based on their profitability (achievement scores). This seems a less-than-compelling rationale, since no stock investor wants to create a portfolio of investments without evidence of future earnings growth or other evidence of increases in stock value. However, and to put it bluntly, nonprofit and for-profit charters and the other "investments" available to districts appear as no better—and perhaps worse—"investments" than traditional public schools. There is no evidence that the strategies of turning over school after school (churn, or creative destruction) or of making public schools compete with contractors will enhance test-based achievement. Although the available evidence on charter schools may not be a reliable indicator of their performance in complex portfolio districts, it is difficult to comprehend how the added stresses and instabilities of closing and opening schools creates an advantage for a charter system. To date, evidence suggests that on the whole, charters perform no better than, and sometimes even worse than, traditional public schools.[53] It is unclear why portfolio advocates would expect better results in a portfolio system.

A second prominent metaphor is that the "government monopoly" of public schooling has "failed," and now it is time to "give the market a chance." This accusation is selectively applied. U.S. schools score on par with other industrialized nations in international comparisons,[54] despite having a uniquely local and unequal funding structure, meaning that the United States is on par despite inadequate public investment in urban districts. This picture is misleading, in that there is strong evidence that in relatively affluent communities, public investment in traditional public schools can and does result in excellence, including excellence in test scores.[55] In the nation's top public schools, per-pupil spending is often several times higher than in the nation's large urban districts, where it is well known that children experience multiple academic disadvantages due to poverty.[56] When declarations of the "failure of public education" are made by advocates of choice and privatization, inevitably these declarations are targeted at urban districts, which are predominantly nonwhite and predominantly poor. In this sense, tinkering with unproven, unstudied, market-oriented experiments appears to be an attempt at avoiding equalizing conditions in the most heavily invested-in public schools attended by largely professional-class whites and in the historically disinvested-in urban public schools. As Dorothy Shipps has shown, the history of business-led reform of public schooling in the United States over the course of the twentieth century has proven that "giving the market a chance" in terms of both business leading the past hundred years of unequal reforms and unequal funding linked to private property wealth has resulted in the present inequalities.[57] There is strong evidence based on international comparisons as to the potential positive effects of equalizing funding and resources so that all schools receive investment at the level of the most successful schools.[58]

Evidence to the contrary notwithstanding, the perception that American public schools are an unmitigated disaster has fostered the idea that it is worthwhile to try anything, including the most radical experiments, to improve U.S. public education. With discussions so dominated by business metaphors, "free market" methods have appeared particularly attractive, including teacher pay for grades (pay for performance) and contracted school management (contracting out). What is more, the business paradigm requires numerically measurable progress, so that test-based achievement comes to completely dominate pedagogy and curriculum. This kind of "bottom line" perspective not only elevates test scores to the highest educational value but also may result in crowding out traditional ways of thinking about and defining education as an intellectual endeavor that involves investigation, debate, and deliberation. A concern with students' ability to think more deeply is replaced by a concern with how to produce higher test scores.

With no positive evidence for either the portfolio district approach or any of its constituent elements, and negative evidence for some elements, one is inclined to invoke Hippocrates' dictum of "First, do no harm" to those considering implementing these radical approaches.

Recommendations

Although the portfolio model is advocated by some policy centers, is implemented in some large urban districts, and appears to be supported by the Obama administration, no peer-reviewed studies of portfolio districts exist, meaning that no reliable empirical evidence about portfolio effects is available to support either the implementation or rejection of the portfolio district model. Nor is such evidence likely to be forthcoming, since even advocates acknowledge the enormous difficulty of designing credible empirical studies to determine how the portfolio approach impacts student achievement and other outcomes. One portfolio district, New Orleans, has produced anecdotal reports of achievement gains. The New Orleans results have, however, been subjected to serious challenge. In addition, available piecemeal evidence and literature from the supporters of the model suggest that the approach is expensive to implement and has unknown to negative effects on student achievement. Finally, extrapolation of research on constituent elements is unreliable, given complex interactions within a portfolio model; even there, however, no evidence is available that the portfolio model will produce gains in achievement or fiscal efficiency.

In light of these considerations, it is recommended that legislators and administrators use great caution in considering the portfolio district approach. It is also highly recommended that before adopting such a strategy, decision makers ask the following questions.

What credible evidence do we have, or can we obtain, that suggests advantages for the portfolio model? What would those advantages be, when might they be expected to materialize, and how might they be documented?

If constituent elements of the model (such as charter schools and test-based accountability) have not produced advantages outside of portfolio systems, what is the rationale for expecting improved outcomes as part of a portfolio system?

What funding will be needed for startup, and where will it come from?

What funding will be necessary for maintenance of the model? Where will continuation funds come from if startup funds expire and are not renewed?

What potential political and social conflicts seem possible? How will concerns of dissenting constituents be addressed?

How will the cost/benefit ratio of the model be determined?

CHAPTER THREE
WHITE COLLAR, RED TAPE

THE NEW MARKET BUREAUCRACY IN CORPORATE SCHOOL REFORM

Introduction

Corporate school reform casts educational problems through business terminology, metaphors, and ideology.[1] Thus, it positions its reforms in ideological terms that its proponents present as apolitical, neutral, and of universal value. Students and parents become consumers of private educational services rather than public citizens. Public school administrators are imagined as private sector managers, CEOs, and entrepreneurs rather than public servants dedicated to the public interest. Teachers become delivery agents of discreet bits of knowledge treated as commodities rather than as public intellectuals responsible for fostering in students the knowledge, skills, and dispositions necessary to link knowledge to broader public issues and social struggles. Tragically and dangerously, corporate school reform eviscerates the development of democratic forms of public schooling that can teach, encourage, and animate public thought, critical citizenship, critical consciousness, and engaged public participation. These public aspects of public schooling are of dire importance as public culture in the United States becomes increasingly marked by irrationalism in numerous domains. As corporate models of reform intensify at the expense of a vibrant political culture, irrationalism takes over.

The broader culture of irrationalism represents a changing relationship between the public and knowledge. The liberal democratic ideal of a citizen armed with knowledge to act in the public arena is increasingly imperiled as the quality of information throughout the public sphere and the capacity of citizens to evaluate information are both in crisis. Corporate media consolidation has resulted in the near death of investigative journalism while the majority of news content is now public relations and nearly all (95 percent) online news is taken from what remains of traditional newspapers.[2] Citizens are inundated with a vast barrage of information and "edutainment" while most have little sense of how to access or evaluate the quality of information as television punditry, unvetted websites and blogs, advertising, and public relations compose the vast majority of news content—and the vast majority of news punditry is from the political right.[3] At a time in which the credible and the outlandish appear indistinguishable to many, and editorial processes are rendered archaic, citizens do not have the tools with which to interpret and make sense of the world they experience. Irrationalism has come to dominate political and public discourse in the form of conspiracy theory, hearsay and anecdote, propaganda, marketing fantasies, "infotainment," and emotionally potent simplifications. September 11 conspiracy plots, birther secrets, medical conspiracy against vaccinations, secret chemicals in our drinking water causing the obesity epidemic, God's plot against homosexuals, and the like, have taken on greater prominence as social and historical explanations, research and science are treated as equivalent to rumor, speculation, and opinion unsupported by evidence and argumentation.

In this context the continued upward redistribution of wealth and inequality in income and the decline of upward mobility and life chances, the violence of poverty, corporate capture of the public sphere, and political exclusion become explained through emotionally potent simplifications that have been readily provided by corporate media culture.

This crisis of legitimation for quality information is matched by a crisis of critical interpretive tools. The rise of irrationalism represents a public and a popular educational crisis. As public education has an important role to play in providing citizens with the intellectual tools of rational discourse, deliberation, and engagement, public education is being radically remade by corporate school reform in ways that hinder critical thought, the evaluation of knowledge, and the relationship between claims to truth and the social forces informing their production. Interested knowledge in the form of public relations is presented as disinterested news in mass media while in concert in public education ever more public relations and advertising invades the classroom in the form of school commercialism, sponsored educational materials, and "lessons" in consumption.[4] As political and material interests seep into every last corner of public culture outside the classroom, inside the classroom the culture (or cult) of standardized testing and standardized curriculum insists that there are no politics to the curriculum or to pedagogy. Corporate school reform expands irrationalism under the guise of a hyper-rationalism in which that which is deemed worthy of knowing is only that which can be numerically quantified. The crucial point is that at a time when it is imperative for citizens to understand the cultural politics and political economic forces animating representations and undergirding claims to truth, classroom pedagogy and curriculum are being overtaken by corporate school reform that posits false claims to neutrality and that denies the politics of knowledge, teaching, and learning. It is not just standardized testing implicated in the dangerous denial of politics but the broader phenomenon of what I call "the new market positivism" at work in reducing all questions of knowledge, teaching, and learning to that which is numerically quantifiable and measurable. Recourse to numbers in the new educational context takes on the guise of science while in fact it furthers irrationalism as knowledge is decontextualized and understanding is misrepresented as a collection of a "world of facts," as if these facts do not require interpretive frameworks and underlying theoretical assumptions.[5]

In the context of a rising irrationalism, mysticism, and public culture dominated by image and fleeting opinion, numbers promise the allure of certainty, the suggestion of scientific solidity.[6] As I will discuss, the institutionalization of high-stakes standardized tests offers the promise and the sheen of solidity and certainty in a world rendered abstract through the principle of capitalist exchange applied everywhere.[7] Under the sway of neoliberal ideology, the suggestion that there is no alternative to the market has produced what Mark Fisher calls "market Stalinism," in which the appearance of market efficiency trumps real efficiency.[8] Such market Stalinism represents a world in which all that is solid melts into public relations—a world in which, as David Simon's television series *The Wire* accurately captured, the game of "juking the stats" (creating foremost an appearance of ever-improving numerical measures of efficiency) comes to supersede reason or rationale grounded in public interest for the policies and practices of teachers and administrators, police officers, politicians, business people, and public workers. As the numbers game seeks to produce ever-better numbers, the pursuit of numbers above all else results in multiple perversions of institutional values and purpose foreclosing the potential for democratic social relations. This is happening in public education under the guise of promoting "market-based efficiencies" by cutting through "public sector bureaucratic red tape."

As the prior chapters have illustrated, although corporate school reform has failed on its own terms of test-based performance, costs, and bureaucracy reduction and though it threatens critical and public education, corporate school reformers have succeeded spectacularly in reframing debates about education in the academic, policy, and public realms in privatized ways. Like the series of pro-privatization, anti-union propaganda films *Waiting for Superman*, *The Lottery*, and *The Cartel* and the steady stream of the same on NBC television, claims do not follow from evidence.[9] These examples suggest more than a stunning irrationality and hypocrisy at the core of the corporate educational reform agenda. Instead, the championing of privatization relies centrally on business metaphors of "efficiency" through "debureaucratization," "competition," "choice," "monopoly," and "failure," the intersecting discourses of market "discipline" and corporeal "discipline." This chapter challenges the use of the metaphors of "market efficiency" achieved by cutting through "bureaucratic red tape." Corporate school reformers have justified numerous forms of privatization, including chartering, contracting, and vouchers, on the basis of cutting through the bureaucratic inefficiencies of the public sector.

One of the most important foundational metaphors for public school privatization that has been promoted since the early 1990s involves claims of the "natural efficiencies of markets" and cutting through bureaucratic red tape. This argument against the alleged bureaucratic inefficiency of the public sector and for the alleged managerial efficiency of the private sector was launched by John Chubb and Terry Moe's *Politics, Markets, and America's Schools* in 1990.[10] Since the publication of this neoliberal educational bible, the de-bureaucratizing force of privatization has been promoted relentlessly in educational policy, despite a lack of evidence for it. Yet, corporate school reforms, rather than decreasing bureaucracy and increasing efficiencies in public schooling, have in fact vastly expanded bureaucracy and created economic and operational inefficiencies. That is, corporate school reform has produced a *privatized bureaucratic infrastructure* that has yet to be identified as such. Moreover, the question of expanding or shrinking bureaucracy to a great extent conceals the ways that corporate school reforms achieve the redistribution of control and governance over policy and practice, curriculum, and administration as well as the redistribution of control over educational resources by creating a new two-tiered system that is privatized at the bottom and undermining the public and critical possibilities of public schools.

This chapter details the new market bureaucracy in corporate school reform to show not only that corporate school reform has failed at the central aim of bureaucracy reduction but also that it smuggles into schooling an entirely new, largely unstudied kind of privatized bureaucracy with high social costs. This chapter provides new conceptual tools by drawing on and building on the literature critiquing the ideology of positivism and social and cultural reproduction in the 1970s and 1980s. The first section revisits the literature of the hidden curriculum, the critique of positivism, and reproduction theory. The second section elaborates on the new market bureaucracy, explaining what is new and different about positivist ideology and social and cultural reproduction today in contrast to in the era of the hidden curriculum and reproduction under Fordism. The third section focuses on how the new market bureaucracy is found in contemporary educational reforms, followed by a section explaining how the new market bureaucracy is involved in producing a new kind of privatized two-tiered educational system that rejects the egalitarian aspirations of the civil rights movement and the Great Society. The chapter aims to identify what has yet to be named as the "new market bureaucracy" at the center of corporate school reform and to encourage empirical research into the new market bureaucracy so that citizens have a better grasp of how to smash the private bureaucracies and expand public, egalitarian, and democratic forms of control and oversight over public schooling.

Situating the New Market Bureaucracy: Hidden Curriculum, Critique of Positivism, and Reproduction Theory in the 1970s and 1980s

Despite the liberal and conservative consensus, public schools are neither neutral providers of educational services nor are they primarily instruments for the inclusion of students into a fundamentally just economy, political system, and culture. Instead, public schools are sites of both ideological indoctrination and ideological and material struggle. As sites of ideological indoctrination, schools teach docility, subjection to authority, and ways of seeing the world through the lens of powerful people and institutions. They too often encourage students to describe and criticize the world within the language and assumptions of the powerful, which today is dominated by the ideologies of corporate culture. Increasingly, public schools are being taken from public ownership and control and being pillaged by profiteers for the private accumulation of capital. This is being done through privatizations, commercialism, and the imperative to install corporate culture throughout schools and school systems. But as sites of ideological and material struggle, public schools are also places that can become more public: they can, for example, be a model for common ownership and control and the fostering of collective democratic control over other institutions, but they also can be places that foster public culture and teach the skills and dispositions for creative democracy in which citizens learn to remake the society they inhabit rather than to simply become assimilated into it.

In the 1970s and 1980s radical educational theorists challenged the mid-twentieth-century conservative historical legacy of educational policy and practice that was grounded in an administrative, bureaucratic, industrial efficiency model of Taylorism and psychological control models such as behaviorism that dominated education in academic and policy arenas.[11] These radical educators sought to revive the progressive educational traditions of John Dewey and George Counts with their emphasis on social reconstruction and the possibilities of public education as a site where a broader democratic culture could be fostered. The radical educators added to the progressive tradition a nondoctrinaire Marxian analysis of class reproduction and the role of schools in replicating economic hierarchies. They drew on and complicated the social and cultural reproduction theories of Louis Althusser, Pierre Bourdieu, and Samuel Bowles and Herbert Gintis, debating the limitations of reproduction theory, including its mechanistic tendencies, its overemphasis on economic determination, and its delimitations of agency, mediation, and culture as a primary social force.

The radical educators in the 1970s and 1980s argued for the political possibilities of student resistance and subaltern cultural formation, and they developed radical pedagogical approaches, much of which drew on the critical pedagogy of Brazilian educator Paulo Freire. In particular, Henry Giroux and Stanley Aronowitz drew heavily on the work of the Frankfurt School of Critical Theory to criticize the culture and ideology of positivism fostered in public schools. Their writing on positivism not only contributed to imagining public schools as sites for the expansion of broader social relations of equality and justice but also proved a trenchant theoretical intervention in response to an era in which the public bureaucracy was described as providing for capital with a "hidden curriculum." This hidden curriculum taught students the social relationships, ideologies, and dispositions necessary for the reproduction of capital. Learning to submit to the authority of the teacher, for example, taught the child to learn to submit to the authority of the boss. Among a number of traditions, the radical theorists of the 1970s and 1980s drew on the insights of Antonio Gramsci's theory of hegemony, which emphasized that every political relationship is an educational one and focused on the cultural struggle for civil society.[12] They appropriated Raymond Williams's insights into the cultural struggle over canon formation that he described as the selective tradition.[13] They built on Pierre Bourdieu's explanation of the forms of capital,[14] wherein he explained the durability of the transmission of class privilege through economic capital, cultural capital, and social capital.[15]

Critical pedagogy's criticism of positivism (drawn from the insights of the Frankfurt School of Critical Theory) offered insights into how the knowledge taught in schools was claimed to be universally valuable and neutral rather than partial, that is, class and culturally based. Hence, the class-based struggles over culture, knowledge, values, interests, and ideologies in schools were concealed through such mechanisms as testing that naturalized, neutralized, and universalized class and culturally specific knowledge. Standardized testing sanctified and contributed to the reproduction of class and cultural hierarchy while framing social inequality as principally a matter of individual merit and natural ability. As well, the Frankfurt School countered the conservative cultural canon and a deeply entrenched educational consensus that presumed that the knowledge and culture of the best and brightest needed to be transmitted to students who would accumulate this knowledge and culture. The Frankfurt School shared with the reproduction theorists a recognition of the extent to which knowledge is grounded in class-based ideologies. However, the Frankfurt School also offered a theory of individual mediation and the possibilities of critical consciousness that differed markedly from the reproduction theorists. The radical pedagogues of the 1970s and 1980s saw radical criticism on its own as inadequate for transforming school practices and the social order. Giroux in particular emphasized the need for theories of agency and possibility that would complement the politically paralyzing domination-oriented view of subject formation (such as the reproduction theories of Bourdieu and Althusser) that tended to produce despair by painting a picture of the social world in which individuals are determined and largely effects of the structural machinery of power.[16]

Part of what the Frankfurt School criticism of positivism offered critical pedagogy was criticism of schooling in a state capitalist bureaucracy that carried forward epistemological assumptions grounded in the enlightenment dream of total knowledge, the faith in technological progress to achieve this end, and—

most importantly—the logic of positivism itself. Positivism separates claims to truth from the values and assumptions underlying the organization and selection of truth claims. Positivism has a hostility to theory, opting instead for a version of social reality through aggregating empirically observable facts. In this view truth is ideally measurable, numerically quantifiable, neutral, and objective. Positivism puts forward a radical objectivism in which the subjective positions of the claimant to truth should not be considered in relation to the truth claim. While retaining a commitment to reason the Frankfurt School challenged central elements of enlightenment rationality, proposing instead dialectical and dialogic engagements with truth claims. The criticisms of positivism and instrumental rationality, represented most centrally by Theodor Adorno, Max Horkheimer, Jürgen Habermas, and Herbert Marcuse, offered the critical education theorists ways of thinking about the relationships between schooling and subject formation, work, leisure, sexuality, psychology, and public life. As opposed to positivism, the dialectical approach of critical theory suggested that the partial knowledge gained in particular institutions needed to be comprehended in terms of the social totality. In other words, school curriculum, teacher and student practices, policy, and administrative rationales could only be comprehended in relation to the broader social structures and relations of power informing these formations. Moreover, critical theory held a promise of the development of a subject imbued with critical consciousness who could learn to interpret, theorize, and ultimately intervene in public problems, challenge domination, and imagine yet unimagined emancipatory social relations and individual ways of living. The dialectical approach of critical theory held that the subject was, on the one hand, formed through ideology and yet, on the other hand, could not be understood as only an effect of ideology.[17]

Critical pedagogy of the 1970s and 1980s continued to hold out a vision of a society of critical philosophical subjects capable of theorizing their experience and the society and imbued with the intellectual tools and dispositions to act and intervene against oppression and for potentially yet unimagined just social arrangements. The promise of the rational autonomous emancipated subject who could be an agent of social transformation was maintained by the critical theorists and stands in contrast to a number of poststructural constructivist positions that deemphasize or even eradicate altogether rational subjectivity, agency, and the educational project of critical pedagogical theory and practice for critical consciousness formation.[18] Theorists of the hidden curriculum and reproduction theory provided a much-needed antidote to the radical subjectivism represented by psychologically oriented academic teacher education programs as well as phenomenologically oriented educational theory that erred on the side of untheorized individual experience. In addition, these critical theorists countered the radical objectivism of the empiricist sociologists of education, who aimed to eradicate theory and reduce educational understandings to counting.

The radical pedagogy criticism of positivism in the late 1970s and early 1980s came at the tail end of the Fordist economy and the shift to post-Fordist regimes of accumulation and complementary neoliberal ideology. This shift marked a transition from the stable, unionized industrial economy, Keynesianism, and the compromise between labor and capital to a financially based service economy in which unionized labor was shipped overseas and labor precarity became increasingly dominant, along with neoliberal economic doctrine emphasizing monetarism, financialization, privatization, and deregulation. This shift also marked a steady decline of direct state provision of caregiving social programs to a state that would increasingly orchestrate and facilitate the entry of private for-profit forces into public services. This shift is exemplified by the dismantling of the employment safety net in the form of welfare and its replacement by workfare, the dismantling and privatization of public housing into for-profit mixed finance developments, the privatization of the military through the extensive use of mercenary contractors, the privatization of public hospitals and health services, the privatization of prisons, and the privatization of schools in the form of charters, vouchers, commercialism, contracting, and the expansion of the ideology of corporate culture to all aspects of school practice and policy.

Fordist forms of self- and social regulation involved time- and labor-intensive approaches to control.[19] The talking cures of psychology and psychiatry in Fordism gave way to the post-Fordist direct bodily controls of psycho-pharmacology. The panopticon of the prison as a place for learned rehabilitation through surveillance gave way to the synoptic prison (such as supermax) in which the prisoner's body is controlled with no expectation or care by authorities about rehabilitation, understood as time-intensive learned self-regulation.[20] The student in post-Fordism has been increasingly made into a corporate subject of these control technologies and a subject of corporeal control. Poor and working-class students in post-Fordism have become subject to an increasingly carceral atmosphere in which close control of the body is paramount. This carceral control intersects with the expansion into schools of corporate-produced security apparatus such as identification cards and metal detectors, and corporate-produced curriculum programs and pedagogical methodologies such as rigid and scripted lessons, corporately managed charter schools deploying rigid prescriptive pedagogies and curriculum (KIPP and EdisonLearning typify these rigid and often scripted approaches),[21] and corporate-produced and -administered rigid and prescriptive remediation methods (supplemental educational services) targeting students who found the rigid and prescriptive pedagogies and curriculum programs uninspiring, boring, and meaningless.

Meanwhile, professional-class students are also subject to corporate/corporeal controls of a different kind. Educated to understand themselves primarily as entrepreneurial subjects, they learn they must compete with the assistance of various pharmacological aids for increasing attention and memory to staying awake to do school work. These pharma-discipline tools offer a medico-therapeutic legitimacy to performance enhancement. Such pharmaceutically enhanced competition is illicit and often illegal in the realm of professional sports, as witnessed by numerous Olympic, bicycling, and baseball doping scandals. Professional-class students learn that they must self-administer the instruments of bodily control for educational and, later, economic competition.[22] Professional-class expectations for students to enter the leadership role of the corporation have meant the deployment of corporate/corporeal control in different forms. The shift from Fordism to post-Fordism revised the relationship between the state and the market. Social regulation moved away from the liberal welfare state and toward privatized and market-oriented policies with the rise of neoliberal ideology and its treatment of every social sphere as a market.

The new state apparatuses in post-Fordism took increasingly privatized forms with the expansion of the privatized medical industry and the decline of public health care, the privatized prison, the dismantling and privatization of public housing, and the privatized school. In post-Fordism, self-regulation for professional managerial subjects took an increasingly individualized form in the imperative for the entrepreneurial self competing in an individualized society. In this context, the hidden curriculum of Fordism, which taught all students the social relationships for the reproduction of capital, was rendered increasingly into a visible and overt curriculum. By the early 1980s public and policy discourse on public education was rapidly being remade overtly through the lens of economic interests and rationales. The *A Nation at Risk* report in 1983 marked an explicit statement of educational purpose defined through global economic competition and equating educational improvement for economic ends as a national security issue.

As neoliberal discourse expanded through educational policy and thought, academically the criticism of positivism was eclipsed by the advent of postmodern theory, identity politics, and the waging of the culture wars in the late 1980s and early 1990s. At the same time, the academic left became particularly en-amored with French cultural theory such as that of Derrida, Foucault, and then Deleuze and Baudrillard, who opened ways of engaging culture and power. Multiculturalism in its various forms, which began as a grassroots movement, ultimately became a hegemonic perspective in its liberal manifestations in colleges of teacher education and educational literature while not necessarily becoming commonplace in actual classroom pedagogy. Critical variants of multicultur-alism (exemplified by Sleeter and Grant, McLaren, Macedo, Bartolome, and Leistyna) remained squarely focused on power and politics and lent themselves to the critique of positivism, yet these approaches were marginal in academic educational studies relative to liberal multiculturalism, defined as tolerance for cultural difference or identity politics oriented toward political pluralism. These latter liberal views largely ignored the intersections of culture with class and as such had no place for comprehending the ways culture is lived through class and class lived through culture, nor the ways that social structures such as capitalism and broader ideologies such as positivism function pedagogically to produce values, identifications, and subject positions.

Despite the various moves away from the criticism of positivism and instru-mental rationality by the Frankfurt School and those who made use of it, as education in the United States became thoroughly subject to the lens and logic of economic rationality, the role of schools, ways of thinking about knowledge, and pedagogical approaches increasingly called for a way of making sense of the new terrain of schooling. On the one hand, the criticism of positivism could not be more relevant today as positivism dominates administration, pedagogy, financial governance, and so on. On the other hand, there is much that is new and different today in how capitalist ideology pervades education from the 1970s and 1980s.

It is not enough to identify the number of connected factors that have given rise to the success of capitalist ideology: the steady and successful cultural project of the right known as neoliberal ideology; the economic project of class warfare that has resulted in concentrations of wealth and income not seen since the Gilded Age; the end of the Soviet sphere as a symbol of an imaginable alterna-tive model to liberal capitalism; the rise of authoritarian capitalism in nations with official Marxist ideology; the concentrated power of corporate media and its unprecedented pedagogical power in the public realm, particularly with regard to educating citizens into consumerism; the erosion of the liberal welfare state in the political arena; and the challenges posed to the liberal intellectual tradition. Positivism remains a crucial ideology for producing assent to an array of unfreedoms by undermining agency, hammering away at the message that alternatives and resistance are impossible, naturalizing the existing unequal order through recourse to scientism.

The most crucial transformation to the public school in the past thirty years is the overt dominance of economic rationales for all educational practices and policies. For liberals and conservatives, nearly everything is justified through two economic promises: the possibility of upward economic mobility and the necessity of global economic competition, which demands educational improvement defined by improvements in numerically quantified test scores. In one sense this has continued the problematic conception of educational equality, defined throughout the twentieth century as the equality of opportunity for access to competition. As Stanley Aronowitz has pointed out, the Deweyan progressive tradition has problematically shared in this attribution of educational opportunity defined as the opportunity of the individual to compete for economic inclusion.[23] In a sense the economization of education simply has made more overt and "honest" the hidden curriculum of capitalist schooling. But at the same time, select liberal humanist referents that founded the public school system have largely been eradicated in the neoliberal era. Gone (with the exception of lip service) is the liberal ideal of the citizen educated as a well-rounded and thoughtful person capable of individual edification, public engagement, and collective self-governance. In a sense, a different part of the liberal philosophical tradition coming from utilitarianism has won out. This is the triumph of *homo oeconomicus*, whose icy calculation for rational self-interest in the marketplace trumps all. Education suffers from a hardened cynicism about the future that Mark Fisher has described as capitalist realism and that Margaret Thatcher described as the TINA thesis—that is, "there is no alternative" to the market.[24] Fisher insightfully discusses how in the neoliberal U.K. educational system, new corporate-style bureaucratic constraints have been imposed on the justification of increased efficiency. The same is true in the U.S. context.

On the basis of efficient delivery of educational services, "deregulation" of public controls has been enacted. Yet, these so-called deregulatory reforms have introduced a vast new regulatory architecture. For example, charter schooling was supposed to free schools and administrators from the bureaucratic constraints of districts to allow for greater accountability (typically this means increased standardized test scores) and decreased costs. Studies of charters have found lower standardized test–based performance than comparative traditional district schools, and the EMOs that manage charters have higher costs allocated to administration.[25] In addition, the charter movement (and "choice" more generally) has introduced entirely new layers of bureaucracy into the school system, such as public-relations schemes to market schools to parents; entire new organizations at the local, state, and national levels to grease the entry of charters into districts; and "research" centers churning out dubious advocacy (as detailed in Chapter 2, the Center on Reinventing Public Education is exemplary), reports, and "studies" to push the various aspects of the privatization agenda. This is to say nothing of the vast new in-school bureaucratic impositions on teachers and administrators who have been transformed into paper-pushing "edupreneurs" encouraged to be constantly hustling for private money to maintain basic operations. The crucial insight to be gleaned from this is that in the name of efficiency, bureaucracy has not been eliminated or necessarily even reduced but rather has resulted in a shift in governance and control of school operations and policy formation, subjecting teachers and administrators to an entirely new array of market-oriented bureaucracy. The utterly obvious cost of this shift is that teachers spend their time doing an overwhelming amount of paperwork rather than preparing for lessons or developing as intellectuals. Less obvious are the ways that teaching becomes deskilled and degraded as curriculum is not to be developed but rather delivered. Teaching becomes robotic, less about intellectual development and more about adhering to prescribed methodological approaches. Such prescriptive methodologies also disallow a focus on the specific educational context and student experience, rendering critical pedagogical approaches impossible.[26] Critical pedagogies ideally begin with student experience and educative contexts to foster interpretation of how broader social forces produce these contexts and experiences. Whereas critical pedagogies aim to expand understanding of the production of both knowledge and subjective experience, prescriptive methodologies aim to decontextualize knowledge and reduce comprehension of experience to the individual. Even less obvious are the ways that such deskilling becomes the means for installing conservative ideologies at odds with public and critical forms of schooling.

Neoliberal education cheerleaders such as *New York Times* columnist Thomas L. Friedman lead the public scapegoating of education, suggesting that high U.S. unemployment rates are caused by the failure of teachers and schools to make adequately entrepreneurial workers.[27] Friedman contends that if schools could promote such entrepreneurialism, those workers would not have been fired. In this view the expansion of the "knowledge economy" depends only on creativity and knowledge production. In reality, economic development and entrepreneurialism also require capital—a vast amount of which was destroyed by the speculative economy produced by the neoliberal policies of privatization and deregulation of the past thirty years.

The New Market Bureaucracy in Public Schooling

The new market bureaucracy in public schooling can be divided into at least three categories for conceptual clarity. First, it involves the shift to what I call the "new market positivism"—that is, numerically quantifiable performance outcomes and the bureaucratic apparatuses put in place to control teachers, administrators, and students and to transform curriculum and pedagogy. Second, the new market bureaucracy involves linking the new market positivism to the institutionalization and the funding of entirely new strata of bureaucratic organizations dedicated to furthering the corporate agendas of privatization, deregulation, standardization, charter support organizations, venture philanthropies,[28] district support organizations, and lobbying infrastructure. Third, it imports into public schooling business expenses and rationales that have financial and social costs, such as public relations and advertising required of both public and privatized schools and real estate deals with chartering organizations, as well as funding for market-style competitions for private funds or public funds to implement corporate reforms such as Race to the Top, the Broad Prize, and the Milken Prize. This third form of the new market bureaucracy involves the use of billions of dollars in private foundation money, especially from the large venture philanthropists Gates, Broad, and Walton, to influence and steer public policy. This foundation wealth, which is only possible through tax incentives, effectively redistributes control over public policy to private super-rich individuals. Thus the public pays to give away control over public institutions.[29]

Though the criticism of positivism in Fordist public schooling came and largely went at the end of the Fordist era and the transition to post-Fordism, the culture of positivism (what I call "the new market positivism") has been at the center of the new forms of market-based educational restructuring since the late 1990s. The new market positivism is typified by the reinvigorated expansion of long-standing positivist approaches to schooling: standardized testing, standardization of curriculum, the demand for policy grounded exclusively in allegedly scientific empirically based pedagogical reforms that (unlike science) lack elaborated framing assumptions or adequate theorization, the drumbeat against educational theory and in favor of a practicalism that insists that "facts" speak for themselves and that untheorized experience is the arbiter of truth. The new market positivism signals the use of these long-standing approaches toward the expansion of multiple forms of educational privatization.

In part, what is new and different now is the use of positivism in coordination with corporate/corporeal control: (1) the use of positivism to justify various forms of public school *privatization*—a shift in the ownership and control of public schools but also a shift in the culture of schools, their curricula, and pedagogies; and (2) repression in schools such as militarized and prisonized schooling, efficiency models for poor students and schools that aim at *total control of the body* and that justify expulsion through the failure of the student to be totally controlled—this is the flip side of the singular promise of economic freedom and choice and self-realization through consumption and work. These forms of control are typified by the use of drugs in schools for educational competition.

For richer students the corporeal/corporate controls take the form largely of pharma-control medicating students into attention (ADD and ADHD drugs such as Ritalin and Adderall), which is coordinated with educational competition and economic competition. Pharmacological control also is used to medicate students out of depression, panic, and anxiety (various antidepression anti-anxiety drugs, such as Prozac, Paxil, Zoloft, and Xanax). The logic of charter schools is shared by these control approaches: loosen up controls (de-democratize, privatize, de-unionize) but then demand test-based accountability defined through testing (positivism). The new market positivism evinces a new relationship between freedom and "unfreedom." The student is promised the opportunity to be disciplined into being an entrepreneurial subject, to compete educationally in order to compete economically. Pharma-control drugs when not given medically are being used illicitly by students for the very same ends: in order to compete educationally to compete economically.

What is crucially different between the old positivism and the new market positivism is the ways that the old positivism neutralized, naturalized, and universalized social and cultural reproduction under the guise of the public good and the public interest, but also individual values of humanist education. During the Fordist "hidden curriculum" era, the economic role of schooling as a sorting and sifting mechanism for the capitalist economy was largely denied. As Bourdieu and Passeron pointed out, mechanisms such as testing simultaneously stratify based on class while *concealing* how merit and talent stand in for the unequal distribution of life chances.[30] The new market positivism still neutralizes, naturalizes, and universalizes the reproduction of the class order through schooling, but it also openly naturalizes and universalizes a particular economic basis for all educational relationships (schooling for work, schooling for economic competition) while justifying a shift in governance and control over educational institutions to private parties. Database projects, designed to boil down the allegedly most efficient knowledge delivery systems and reward and punish teachers and students, are not only at the center of pedagogical, curricular, and administrative reform but, unlike during the era of the hidden curriculum, are openly justified through the allegedly universal benefits of capitalism. The new market positivism subjects all to standardization and normalization of knowledge, denying the class and cultural interests, the political struggle behind the organization and framing of claims to truth. The trend rejects critical pedagogies that make power, politics, history, and ethics central to teaching and learning and that accord with the values of democratic community. *The new market positivism links its denial and concealment of the politics of knowledge to its open and aggressive application of capitalist ideology to every aspect of public schooling.* The positivism of the hidden curriculum era concealed the politics of knowledge in order to conceal the capitalist ideology structuring public education. Put bluntly, the reproduction of the stratified workforce, the unequal distribution of life chances, and so on were made to appear natural, neutral, and unquestionable in the era of the hidden curriculum, undermining the capacity of public schools to function as critical public spheres. The new market positivism still conceals the politics of knowledge but does so while redefining individual and collective opportunity strictly through open reference to a supreme value on capitalism. The intensified testing, control of time, and standardization regimens of the new market positivism further threaten the possibilities for teachers to teach against the grain (as Roger Simon describes it) and to engage in critical pedagogical practices. The new market positivism effects a kind of deep privatization in the sense that it renders public schools places that are less open to struggle for public values, identifications, and interpretations, thereby reducing the social space of noncommercial values, ideas, and ideologies.

Jeff Edmondson, president of the Strive Together–National Cradle to Career Network, which "partners" with public schools to do turnarounds, is, according to writer David Bornstein, leading a national effort for establishing "data war rooms" in schools for "data driven instruction," "data driven administration," and the like. As Edmondson explains in the *New York Times*, "The key to making a partnership work is setting a common vision and finding a common language. You can't let people get focused on ideological or political issues. You need a common language to bring people together and that language is the data."[31] Edmondson concisely and powerfully describes the denial of politics behind the new market positivism. On the one hand, there is a universal assumption that the aim of such reform is to increase student test scores toward "global economic competition," that is, capitalist inclusion. On the other hand, there is a denial that such an agenda for education is of course profoundly political. Take a particularly glaring class example. Those who own industry and seek to maximize profit by minimizing labor costs do not share a common set of interests, for example, with those workers who will be forced to sell their time and labor power to the owners in a position to exploit it. The politics of labor is perhaps more concretely understood by the fact that Strive Together is affiliated with the organization Stand for Kids, which advocates limiting public teachers' collective bargaining rights in Cincinnati Public Schools, and is linked to Michelle Rhee's New Teacher Project (and National Council on Teacher Quality, NCTQ), which aims for privatization, union busting, pay for test scores, the end of teacher job security, and less educated and less experienced teachers. Data can be creatively manipulated or utterly ignored when in the service of this ideological agenda pushed by Rhee and the New Teacher Project, NCTQ, Hanushek, Finn, Peterson, and the usual cast of corporate school reformers affiliated with Hoover, Fordham, AEI, Heritage, and the other rightist think tanks.[32] Data as "the common language" provides a way to deny the sometimes incommensurably different values, histories, and interests of different groups.

As Mark Fisher details in his book *Capitalist Realism: Is There No Alternative?* the new market bureaucracy that has overtaken public schooling installs an audit culture in which it is not performance of teachers and students that is compared but rather "comparison between the audited representation of that performance and output."

> The idealized market was supposed to deliver "friction free" exchanges, in which the desires of consumers would be met directly, without the need for intervention or mediation by regulatory agencies. Yet the drive to assess the performance of workers and to measure forms of labor which, by their nature, are resistant

> to quantification, has inevitably required additional layers of management and bureaucracy.... Inevitably, a short circuiting occurs, and work becomes geared towards the generation and messaging of representations rather than to the official goals of the work itself.[33]

As numerical test output targets become the end of schooling in the new market bureaucracy, as Fisher puts it, "if students are less skilled and knowledgeable than their predecessors, this is due not to a decline in the quality of examinations per se, but to the fact that all of the teaching is geared towards passing the exams. Narrowly focused 'exam drill' replaces a wider engagement with subjects."[34] Fisher observes that more effort ends up expended on generating and representing the "outputs," which in education take the form of manipulated test data, than on improving the quality and depth of instruction—that is, the process of teaching itself.

Theodor Adorno's concept of what drives the allure of positivism is the promise of the concrete in the world of abstraction/alienation produced by a social world characterized by market exchange in which everything is turned into equivalences.[35] What we have now is a new, ever more controlled and output-oriented educational system in which numbers allegedly dictate. Yet we have policy implementation that is utterly at odds with both empirical evidence for reforms (charters and EMOs) within the positivist assumptions, and we have the public purposes of schooling being elided by these control- and output-oriented bureaucratic reforms, along with an explicit justification of all policy on the basis of individual participation in capitalism—a system represented as the only game in town not just economically but politically and culturally as well. The triumph then, as Fisher points out, is an ascendancy of schooling as public relations in which everyone knows the lie but plays along anyway. As charters and EMOs show test scores that are worse or on par with traditional public schools, those at the center of the audit culture (such as the venture philanthropists Gates and Broad) change the audit criteria from standardized test scores to graduation and college enrollment rates.[36] Crucial to the public assenting to such policies is continuously produced pedagogies that educate subjects ideologically and that also foster a culture of cynicism about intervening to challenge the audit culture and the new market positivism.

We need to rethink the accusations of bureaucratic "red tape" that have been a core part of the corporate reform agenda. What most teachers and administrators experience in schools is a new market bureaucracy that has been installed and expanded under the guise of market efficiencies. Fisher offers a succinct and powerful antidote to the new market bureaucracy. He calls for demanding fulfillment of the promises for debureaucratization instilled through neoliberalism. In other words, we should take the neoliberal imperative for cutting bureaucratic red tape seriously but direct this imperative toward market-driven audit culture. In education, this means aiming to dismantle the market bureaucracy and its frenzied pursuit of evermore numerical representations of educational progress.

The new market positivism appears in the "global knowledge economy" mantra in a two-part argument. First, the allegedly universally valuable test scores (such as the OECD PISA international comparisons in reading, math, and science) are used to claim that the public school system has failed, and that failure both explains the current failure of capitalism to provide adequate employment growth and portends a bleak future as other nations competing against the United States on tests threaten U.S. economic and technological hegemony. Yet, as an atypical article, "U.S. Schools Are Still Ahead—Way Ahead," in the business press points out, these stereotypes about the failures of U.S. public schooling do not stand up to evidence, including the ones about international test score comparisons, the quality of science and engineering preparation, and worries about U.S. students socializing instead of studying hard.[37] As Vivek Wadhwa rightly argues, the differences between the United States and other nations are negligible; while the United States has the greatest diversity in student population ("disadvantaged minorities and unskilled immigrants") and still produces more higher performing students in science and reading than any other country, in math it comes second only to Japan. The second part of the "global knowledge economy" argument says that this supposed failure demands radical market reforms (charters and other privatizations, linking teacher pay to test scores, crushing teacher unions) despite the fact that no evidence exists for such reforms on the same terms of test-based improvement or in terms of cost savings. Such arguments, which are being rehearsed by the U.S. Secretary of Education, the venture philanthropists, and the mass media, suggest that what is at play in the new market positivism is a change in the relationship between truth and authority with regard to evidence and empirical data.

While the logic of empiricism has overtaken educational debates, demanding that everything be justified with an evidentiary basis, in reality the reforms are being implemented principally through the justification of market ideologies and metaphors that most often run contrary to the evidence of proponents. Whether it is charter schools, for-profit management companies, vouchers, so-called portfolio districts, NCLB, or competitions like Race to the Top, implementation is based not on evidence but on market advocacy. The new market positivism is characterized by a triumph of irrationalism under the guise of rationality; a new bureaucracy under the guise of efficiency; audit culture and unaccountability at the top masquerading as accountability; extension of repressive bodily and hierarchical institutional controls defended through reference to freedom and opportunity; anti-intellectualism and destruction of the conditions for creativity pushed on the basis of the need to produce creatively minded workers and entrepreneurs; and a denial of intellectual process, curiosity, debate, and dialogue justified on the basis of intellectual excellence. There is a kind of emptiness at the core of the new market positivism in that it is seldom about making decisions based on the imperative for empirical evidence and conceptual justification and more about using evidence when convenient for the ends of amassing elite control. In education, corporate bureaucracy is being installed and expanded, yet as Wall Street is discovering, corporate bureaucracy may have seen its best days. The editor of the *Wall Street Journal*, Alan Murray, in August 2010 argued that "corporate bureaucracy is becoming obsolete."[38] Wall Street subjects teachers and students, administrators and citizens to the sloughed-off detritus of corporate culture. Meanwhile, business prescriptions for education are exactly what business is discarding for business.

The New Market Positivism in the Dominant Educational Reforms

Positivism is at the center of dominant educational reforms that are modeled on corporate culture and a private-sector vision of management, growth, and quality. Standardized testing is at the center of all the following: No Child Left Behind and its blueprint for reauthorization, Race to the Top; the push for value-added assessment; the creation of database tracking projects to longitudinally measure teacher performance on students' standardized tests; the linkage of teacher evaluation and pay to such standardized test–based measures; the imposition of "urban portfolio districts"; legislative moves to stifle the power of teachers' unions; the unbridled entry of corporate managers into school reform by-passing professional educators and educational scholarship; and the use of corporate media to frame educational problems and solutions. Standardized testing has also been at the center of the push for charter school expansion and the expansion of for-profit management companies running schools.

These dominant reforms share a common logic with regard to standardized testing. Test scores that are low in relation to the norm are used to justify policies such as regressive funding formulas (NCLB), imperatives for corporate reforms like "turnarounds" (NCLB and Race to the Top), school closures (NCLB and Race to the Top), and school privatizations. Corporate reformers use the alleged objectivity of the standardized tests to champion corporate reforms that lack scholarly or empirical justification. This alleged objectivity dooms the public schools under scrutiny, but the reforms put forward by the corporate reformers are not held to the same standards. For example, charter schools, No Child Left Behind, and for-profit management of schools can be fairly described as "failed" corporate educational reforms that do not increase standardized test scores, and no evidence for the success of turnarounds and portfolio districts exists (see Chapter 2). Indeed, the proponents of portfolio districts—which model districts on a stock portfolio and the superintendent as a stock investor—contend that it is impossible to measure the success of such models in terms of the same standardized testing that they use to justify implementation.

As the corporate reforms have failed to succeed on the proponents' grounds (higher test scores), proponents have responded with two strategies. The first is willful ignorance. Policy elites such as the Secretary of Education, the venture philanthropists, charter school associations, and right-wing think tanks have continued, for example, to wrongly assert the success of charters and for-profit management companies and to insist on the need to continue NCLB (albeit slightly tweaked). The other strategy has been to change the rules of the game. This has been most evident with the failure of the charter movement to prove itself in terms of the test score improvements that justified its corporate backers. With a lack of test-based evidence, a number of policy makers have come out suggesting other measures to determine charters a success. Eugenicist, Harvard professor, and co-author of the *Bell Curve*, Charles Murray, wrote explicitly about the need to change the measure in a *New York Times* op-ed.[39] Charters, it seems, were justified for implementation based on the low test scores of public schools, but the same criteria should not be used to justify their continuation. Likewise, Paul Hill, who leads the pro-privatization Center on Reinventing Public Education at the University of Washington, explained in his reports on creating portfolio districts that the measure of the success of charters and other privatizations should be the implementation of these reforms rather than the rise in test scores.[40] The Bill and Melinda Gates Foundation has been the single largest funder of charter school expansion for schools, districts, and numerous charter "support" organizations at the local, state, and national levels. Since succeeding in getting the dubious charter movement made a central element of the federal education agenda in Race to the Top and NCLB, the Gates Foundation's reauthorization efforts have never admitted that evidence does not back its billions in spending. Instead, it continues to pour money into charters and other reforms more closely tied to standardized testing. For example, the foundation is pushing to expand value-added assessment and to link it to teacher pay, and to link value-added assessment to video surveillance. These reforms aim to deduce a methodology for teaching practice that will raise test scores and that can be forced on numerous teachers.

New market positivism can also be found in the market-based rearticulation of the language of schooling for social justice. While Secretary of Education Arne Duncan regularly describes education as the most important social justice and civil rights issue today, he asserts that the imperatives for test-based measures of educational quality and privatizations are the solution to the historical injustices he registers. Duncan is not alone. The Gates and Broad foundations explain their push for test-based reforms, especially database tracking of student tests scores, as intended to "close the achievement gap." Duncan, Gates, Broad, and other proponents of the new market positivism share a number of related assumptions about knowledge, the self, and society. In their view, knowledge should be efficiently delivered and does not need to be comprehended in relation to its conditions of production or interpretation. In other words, the subjective positions of the claimant of truths do not need to be investigated, nor do the objective conditions that give rise to particular interpretations need to be comprehended. In this static view of knowledge, the self ought to accumulate knowledge toward the end of "measurable achievement" and instrumental action linked to economic utility. Within this view, social justice is not to be achieved by collective action and aspirations for reconceptualizing and impacting the social world. Instead, social justice for the new market positivists becomes an individualized pursuit in which disciplined consumption of preordained knowledge creates the possibilities for inclusion into a social order presumed to be fundamentally just. Of course, this has little to do with social justice in the sense of transforming the economy by ameliorating the devastating effects and dire inequalities of wealth and income of capitalism through social democratic welfare state controls. Nor does it have to do with more fundamentally transforming the political governance of capitalism through democratizing relations of production and consumption. As well, this conception of social justice has no sense of transforming the culture to value dissent, disagreement, difference, and dialogue, which are the lifeblood of democratic social relations. Instead, this version of social justice imposes a singular value of individual economic inclusion in a corporate economy.

The ubiquitous concepts of "student achievement," the "achievement gap," and the call across the political spectrum to "close the achievement gap" all presume that achievement is measured by standardized testing. "Student achievement" naturalizes, neutralizes, and universalizes class- and culturally specific knowledge, establishing norms, comparing, and ranking in relation to the norm, all the while disavowing the politics of knowledge informing the selection and framing of knowledge on the tests. The denial of the politics of knowledge is then further deepened by the concept of the achievement gap, which suggests that the test outcomes indicate how racial and ethnic groups fare in relation to the norm. In the spirit and legacy of cultural imperialism and colonialism, racial and ethnic cultural differences are ignored and denied in the making of the standardized tests but then differences are invoked to demand that the ordained knowledge be consumed and displayed on the tests.[41] In this view, cultural differences and struggles over their meaning are not at the center of teaching and learning an object of analysis that could form the basis for emancipatory pedagogies that comprehend claims to truth in relation to the social positioning of individuals and groups. Instead, cultural differences in the new market positivism are only to be registered as something to be overcome as all students are required to take in the dogma.

The New Market Positivism in the New Two-Tiered Educational System

As David Hursh, Sandra Mathison, and Mark Garrison[42] among others powerfully emphasize, we must understand the emphasis on standardized testing as both utterly central to historical struggles over public education and central to the current neoliberal school reforms. What is afoot in the current privatization initiatives is an attempt to do nothing short of transform public education into a private market, essentially ending public education.

The transformation of public education into a private market is being done by what Naomi Klein calls "disaster capitalism," David Harvey describes as "accumulation by dispossession," and in education I have termed "capitalizing on disaster" or "smash and grab privatization," in which declarations of disaster, failure, and crisis are used to implement long-standing privatization initiatives that could not be otherwise enacted. This broader privatization trend is particularly evident in the rapidly expanding charter movement (which is a frontal assault on teachers' unions, teacher work, and teaching as a critical and intellectual endeavor, and the spear tip of the privatization movement), the continuing voucher movement, Race to the Top, and the organized efforts of the venture philanthropies[43] neoliberal think tanks, associations, and political organizations as well as back-to-back secretaries of the U.S. Department of Education attended by their staff of bureaucrats with a corporate view of school reform.

These organizations and individuals are rapidly succeeding in smashing teachers' unions and overrunning local school boards in order to put in place privatized school networks, as in New Orleans after Hurricane Katrina. Indeed, this great neoliberal experiment in privatization, in which a school district was remade with privatized charter networks, is currently being expanded statewide in Louisiana. Louisiana governor Bobby Jindal, Louisiana Board of Education superintendent Paul Pastorek, and Recovery School District CEO Paul Vallas seek to ratchet up school failure scores to declare more and more public schools as "failed" and subject to closure and replacement by privatized schools. The privatizers have a profound antipathy for teacher education and academically grounded certification, local school boards, and community governance and seem to favor anti-intellectual practicalism, teacher de-skilling, and radical experimentation with unproven market-based reforms.

What the teachers' unions, education scholars, teachers, and everyone concerned about strengthening public education have to grasp is that *as long as the framing of educational quality remains trapped within the current frame of allegedly neutral and allegedly objective quantifiable "student achievement," public education stands to be dismantled.*

The kind of schooling pushed by the privatization advocates aims to transform a current dual system of public schooling into another dual system of public schooling. In the current dual system, elite public schools in rich, predominantly white communities prepare managers, leaders, and professionals for the top of the economy and the state while the underfunded public schools in poor, working-class, and predominantly nonwhite communities prepare the docile, disciplined workforce for the bad jobs at the bottom of the economy or for exclusion from the economy altogether. Despite the ceaseless neoliberal and liberal rhetoric of crisis and failure, the public schools—as Freire, Bourdieu, Ollman, and others recognize—do exactly what they are supposed to do:

they produce the stratified workforce while sanctifying inequality as a matter of individual merit or talent.[44] The neoliberal privatization reforms maintain the dual system, leaving in place the elite public schools but targeting predominantly poor schools and students of color to turn them into short-term profit opportunities in numerous ways. The contracting, testing, and tutoring schemes illustrated by Patricia Burch[45] join with for-profit management and charters, as well as all the ancillary profits that can be generated through privatization, like the public funds that will pour into marketing charter schools to prospective "customers" through advertising, and the lucrative real estate deals that charter schools require.[46] At present the lower end of the dual system provides a deferred investment in low-pay, low-skill disciplined workers and fodder for the for-profit prison industry and the military. Privatization targets the low end of the dual system and pillages the public sector for short-term profits benefitting the ruling class and professional class while doing nothing to transform the dual system of public education into a single system as good as its best parts throughout. For investors in privatization, the benefits are double: money can be made in the short run by draining public tax revenue and can still be produced in the long term with the creation of an exploitable future workforce. And, as the investors are benefitting twice, they can feel good that they are giving poor students "every opportunity" to benefit themselves. As class mobility declines and unemployment and inequality in wealth and income rises, economic inequality is shifted onto students, who will need to be—in the words of Thomas Friedman—more entrepreneurial to get and keep scarcer jobs. This displaces the violence of the capitalist economy onto the weakest and most vulnerable citizens, children. As I write this, one in five U.S. children is on food stamps, and child homelessness is ballooning.[47] The goal should not be to see how we can all help to subsidize the rich getting richer by replicating a more lucrative system of dual education—the rich part still public and the poor part privatized. The goal must be ending the dual education system. But the new market positivism is at the core of creating the new privatized dual education system by making standardized testing, database tracking, and standardization of curriculum and pedagogy the measure of good teaching and learning. Students are increasingly sorted and sifted while the numbers give a guise of neutrality concealing the differential distribution of material and symbolic power. The alternative to these positivist approaches to teaching and learning are democratic approaches to education, such as critical pedagogy. The next chapter takes on the liberal response to corporate school reform to highlight how cultural theory is a central element of both the criticism of corporate school reform and a necessity for putting forward a newly invigorated public democratic form of education.

CHAPTER FOUR
WHY DEMOCRATIC PEDAGOGY IS CRUCIAL FOR CONFRONTING CORPORATE SCHOOL REFORM AND HOW LIBERALS ARE MAKING THINGS WORSE

For more than a decade I and other critical scholars on the left,[1] including Henry Giroux, Michael Apple, Lois Weiner, David Gabbard, Joel Spring, Wayne Ross, and David Hursh, have criticized the corporatization of public schooling, linking the right-wing assault to the broader neoliberal trend and corporate globalization. However, from the 1980s until 2010, few Americans were aware of the extent to which U.S. public schooling was being remade in the image of the corporation. Nor were most Americans aware of the plans of the corporate school reformers essentially to transform one of the largest public sectors into a private industry. Yet, by 2010, as evidence in the policy arena mounted that corporate school reform was showing conclusive signs of being a failure in the terms of its proponents (test scores and costs),[2] a massive public relations and advertising campaign was rolled out in the place of evidence. Three films were released with backing by corporate school reformers: *Waiting for Superman*, *The Lottery*, and *The Cartel*. Each told a story of a "failed" public school system in dire need of market-based solutions. The first two blamed poverty on bad schools, teachers, and teachers' unions and celebrated privately managed charter schools, while the third focused on blaming teachers' unions for everything wrong with public education. The film campaign was joined by a barrage of television coverage (especially by NBC) that told the same story of public-sector failure and private-sector rescue.

The media blitz came as study after study showed that the centerpiece of corporate school reform, charter schools, have done poorly in test-based comparisons with traditional public schools,[3] that they worsen racial segregation,[4] that they push out special-needs students who put pressure on finances and scores,[5] that they drain resources from district schools while failing to address how corporate America has failed public education and gutted the social state,[6] that they depend on philanthropic support that can dry up,[7] and that they are less stable than traditional public schools.[8] The media propaganda also came on the heels of studies showing that the experiments in for-profit companies running schools likewise do not do as well as traditional public schools on test-based comparisons and that they cost more than public schools for administration.[9] As Henry Giroux has emphasized, the antipublic media onslaught came on the heels of one of the largest public sector bailouts of the private sector in history, when the public needed to save corporations (especially financial and automotive companies acting like banks) from themselves. Within two years, these same industries were making record profits as the unemployment rate soared and as politicians set their sights on attacking public-sector workforces, unions, and the pension and health care funds of public workers who had dedicated their lives to public service. In the media, scapegoating teachers became a national pastime. From Thomas Friedman's *New York Times* columns to Federal Reserve Chairman Ben Bernanke's[10] public comments to President Obama's *60 Minutes* interview,[11] education was held as responsible to restore the crippled economy and address soaring unemployment rates. Friedman claimed that if only teachers produced entrepreneurial students, those students would create profits in businesses and not have to be laid off.[12] Mass firings were the result neither of the structural realities of capitalism nor the lack of social state safety nets, or even due to the lack of public employment schemes. They were the fault of teachers.[13]

Such framing is out of touch with the realities of business (e.g., entrepreneurship in this vision requires no capital outlays). Indeed, as Alan Murray, an editor of the *Wall Street Journal*, insists, the corporate form of management that is encumbered by bureaucratic inertia is an organizational model incapable of dealing with change.[14] He looks to Wikipedia and open-source operating systems as examples of complicated systems that thrive without hierarchical corporate management. Yet, as Wall Street is discovering that corporate management has seen its best days and is ready to be retired, conservatives and a surprising number of liberals have accepted the idea that what public education needs is a massive dose of the corporate form of management. After all, so goes the doxa in mass media and policy circles, contrary to the editor of the *Wall Street Journal*, that because markets are always efficient, schools should be subject to corporate forms of management and organization. Of course, public institutions—including public schools—have a fundamentally different mission of serving the public interest than do private sector institutions aiming for profit. Yet, in the standard neoliberal trope, the public sector is imagined as the private sector and exists to serve it as well.

Ideologically, this scapegoating of public education and teachers was a masterful move at refocusing the blame for the economic crisis and its destruction away from the neoliberal economic dogma that produced it: deregulation, privatization, and resource-grabbing wars. The liberal failure to deal with these neoliberal demands and the liberal tendency to view public education as apolitical and neutral essentially colluded with the rightist project to pillage public education and other public services. If, as the liberals increasingly assumed, the only imperative was efficacy of delivery, and the aim was making useful workers and consumers, then contracting out, privatizing, and deregulating were worth a shot.[15] After all, it would be too hard to deal with such fundamental problems of radically unequal funding and segregation.[16]

In 2010 the broader public also became aware of the extent of corporate school reform when Diane Ravitch's book *The Death and Life of the Great American School System* was promoted as a *New York Times* bestseller. Ravitch, who had been assistant secretary of education under George H. Bush and had been at the center of the corporate reform agenda championing privatization as a fellow at prominent right-wing think tanks, had a political "conversion" around 2008 and began palling around with Randi Weingarten, the head of New York City's United Federation of Teachers (AFT affiliate), who would become head of the American Federation of Teachers.

In the course of Ravitch's book, she explains that she was wrong to spend so many years working to expand privatization, charters, vouchers, "choice," and high-stakes standardized testing—a system that rewards high-scoring students with more resources and punishes those students who need the most help. Ravitch reveals that the corporate school reformers are playing a shell game with numbers—both test scores and finances—and she defends the public school system, particularly the neighborhood school. However, she insists that she was never wrong about what she always cared about most—a "strong" curriculum—by which she means a standardized core knowledge curriculum aligned with cultural conservatives such as E. D. Hirsch. This is a view of knowledge that assumes teachers need to transmit "the ideas of the best and the brightest." Still sounding frankly nostalgic for an era of schooling before both multiculturalism and the civil rights movement, Ravitch blames "progressive education," with its democratic values and its focus on pedagogical approaches oriented toward just social progress, for setting the stage for the destruction wrought by the corporate school reformers. For Ravitch, the destruction is primarily about "narrowing" the curriculum. Ravitch's most seemingly radical position against the corporate financial plunder of public schooling yields a position that teachers ought to be activists and work with unions, but still these political struggles outside of classrooms have no connection to what students learn and what should go on in classrooms.[17]

Her position is very much at odds with critical traditions in education,[18] such as Giroux's work, that emphasize that students learn how claims to truth relate to both their own experiences and broader structures of power, that the curriculum is struggled over, and that education is thoroughly political. Unlike the progressive tradition that she blames, Ravitch, like most liberals and conservatives, presumes that curriculum and pedagogy can be politically neutral. Yet, Ravitch actively promotes a conservative cultural canon of core knowledge. Her view is shared by the much-celebrated liberal policy scholar Linda Darling-Hammond, who likewise denies the politics of knowledge, calling for an end to the "curriculum wars," and who defends Hirsch's core knowledge approach. The AFT's Albert Shanker Institute is unfortunately on board with the cultural right promoting the common core standards of the National Governors Association with its high-profile liberal and conservative signatories. The common core standards do not prescribe a common core curriculum, but they set the stage for it by giving standards delinked from curriculum guidelines. As two common core curriculum groups, Core Knowledge (of which Ravitch is a leader) and Common Core, provide the curricular content guidance for the common core standards, two testing companies compete to win a massive federal contract to create the one national common core standardized test. Ravitch aligns herself against the vocationalization agenda of the 21st Century Skills proponents who push basic skills for work as she continues her long-standing project of working to put in place a conservative common core curriculum. Of course, the standards and the curriculum put forward by the common core groups offer little in the way of encouraging students to comprehend how, for example, standardization and standardized testing are big business; who, for example, is claiming the knowledge in the curriculum and on the future tests to be valuable and how they got the social power to enforce it; or what, for example, is missing from these canons, such as the voices from below, the perspectives of the oppressed, and how the knowledge learned relates to the agency of students to work collectively to transform oppressive structures of power.

Although much of Ravitch's criticisms of the corporatization of schools offers valuable information, criticisms of testing and privatization have long been leveled by the aforementioned critical education scholars within a broader analysis of how social inequalities relate to knowledge. However, Ravitch is wrong in ways that have big implications for defending public education and teachers' unions from the corporate assault. She essentially suggests that the biggest threat posed by the corporate agenda is the threat to a conservative common core curriculum. She still blames progressive education for the problems of public schooling, she blames progressives for setting the stage for corporatization, and she sounds frankly nostalgic for a return to the glory days before the civil rights movement and multiculturalism. She remains committed to testing—just not high-stakes testing—and she takes the indefensible position that curriculum and pedagogy are apolitical. Even while she defends the neighborhood school she never questions the de facto privatized funding structure in the United States, which maintains inequality by keeping most school funding tied to local property ownership. Speaking in Chicago at DePaul she insisted that public tax dollars ought to fund the religious schooling of the Catholic church, which is a message that sounds a lot like the support for vouchers she allegedly left behind.

If AFT president Randi Weingarten seemed to have an influence on Ravitch's political "conversion," then perhaps Ravitch in turn can explain how Weingarten and the AFT came out in favor of the common core standards promulgated by the National Governors Association.[19] Such curricular standardization, for which a single national test is being formulated, more deeply institutionalizes the positivism of the corporate approach to knowledge. As teachers and teacher education programs are held "accountable" to this singular body of knowledge, critical pedagogical questions are eradicated from the educational process. Such questions include: Who claims this to be true and why? What are the positions of the makers of the curriculum and the tests, and how do these relate to broader social struggles? What do these claims to truth have to do with what students experience, and what forces and structures produce such experiences? The National Governors Association and Shanker Institute deny that they are promoting rigid approaches to teaching and learning because they encourage the building of "knowledge on knowledge" and only establish guidelines that ultimately encourage "critical thinking." In addition to embracing an archaic and static conception of knowledge in which knowledge is accumulated like money in the bank, they are developing an active rejection of theorizing knowledge—the active and ongoing engagement with the conditions of knowledge production, distribution, and mediation.

As Giroux's work highlights, different historical moments marked by different social struggles offer different economic, political, and cultural formations within which the conditions of dominant knowledge need to be questioned and in which the possibilities for oppositional knowledge change and demand theorization. As Giroux contends, student experience needs to be meaningful in order for it to be made critical so that it can be transformative. This means that learning as the basis for civic literacy must connect the experiences students face to the broader social, structural, and systemic conditions that produce those experiences. The liberal and conservative conception of learning embraces critical thinking as problem solving while eschewing critical pedagogy's understanding of teacher work, curriculum, and pedagogy as political, as part of broader social movements, as theoretical, and as inextricably linked with individual, community, and social transformation. Giroux writes,

> I think critical pedagogy begins with the assumption that knowledge and power should always be subject to debate, held accountable, and critically engaged. Central to the very definition of critical pedagogy is a common concern for reforming schools and developing modes of pedagogical practice in which teachers and students become critical agents actively questioning and negotiating the relationship between theory and practice, critical analysis and common sense, and learning and social change.[20]

The common core standards and curriculum contributes to the assault on teachers' unions, teaching as intellectual work, and tenure as the call becomes deafening for measuring teachers by student test outcomes rather than experience and ongoing development. As long as the union and teachers accept this false measure of educational value, the corporate agenda wins. The only important matters in this framing are the efficacy of delivery, and there is really no way to argue other than to dispute the numbers. Once one accepts these basic assumptions of a false neutrality and universality, then contracting and privatization can be justified, but the aim of education is essentially defined as the efficacious private delivery of a private service.[21]

Ravitch talks a good game about public education for citizenship, but she does not suggest genuinely equalizing funding, desegregating schools, or, most important, making schools places in which students can learn to be the kinds of critical citizens who can remake the society and its institutions. Class and cultural difference and antagonism in her view are problems that should be registered as obstacles only to be overcome, whereas the knowledge, skills, dispositions, and values of dominant groups are universalized as the norm toward which everyone should aspire. Ravitch represents a cultural conservative break with the fiscal conservatives who want to privatize the system and destroy the unions. Although she has been massively promoted on *Democracy Now!*[22] and *The Nation*,[23] these otherwise progressive media venues are not bothering to look closely at what she is writing and to raise the kinds of more serious questions represented by Giroux's scholarship.[24]

Ravitch's leadership in a "Save Our Schools" march on Washington planned for summer 2011 is defined by defending public schools from "political and corporate agendas" and against "resegregating" schools. In this framing the long-standing reality of segregation is denied while public schools are falsely claimed to be apolitical. Furthermore, the corporate takeover of public education is positioned as akin to "political" (read: left) agendas for schools as opposed to the allegedly neutral agenda of Ravitch and her liberal allies. Ravitch turns to activism, but there is no relationship between the politics of the street and the politics of pedagogy and curriculum. She defends a public system that is structured through vast inequality and that is in need of transformation. The transformation, however, if it is to be democratic and public must eschew both the neoliberal corporate assault and the cultural conservatism of Ravitch and Hirsch and instead involve critical pedagogical approaches and a critical conception of curriculum. As Giroux writes,

> Cornelius Castoriadis insightfully argues that for any regime of democracy to be vital, it needs to create citizens who are critical thinkers capable of calling existing institutions into question, asserting individual rights, and assuming public responsibility. In this instance, critical pedagogy as an alternative form of civic education and literacy provides oppositional knowledges, skills, and theoretical tools for highlighting the workings of power and reclaiming the possibility of intervening in its operations and effects. But Castoriadis also suggests that civic literacy must be linked to the task of creating new locations of struggle that offer critical opportunities for experiencing political agency within social domains that provide the concrete conditions in which

people can exercise their capacities and skills "as part of the very process of governing."[25]

Darling-Hammond, like Ravitch, also criticizes, though in a much milder way, the corporate school agenda (though she does not call it that) with its emphasis on high-stakes testing, privatization, union-busting, the undermining of certification and advanced education for teachers, and the replacement of teachers with online education. Darling-Hammond's liberal defense of public schooling offers some tools for responding to the corporate assault, but they are severely limiting.

On February 26, 2011, the *Chicago Tribune* published the editorial "The Next Teacher's Contract" with education recommendations for mayor-elect Rahm Emmanuel. The editorial shares the positions of Wisconsin governor Scott Walker on education, unions, and the public sector. The *Tribune* calls for extending the school day, cutting spending that supports teachers in pursuing advanced degrees or certificates, replacing teachers with online instruction, paying teachers for test outcomes but not seniority, and ending tenure for teachers. Darling-Hammond's book, *The Flat World and Education*, counters these demands. For example, she explains that top-scoring nations have expanded teacher preparation time relative to classroom instruction time. In fact, the United States has teachers in front of students for more time than any other nation but deprives them of much-needed preparation time.[26] In test-score-successful nations, new teachers spend a significant amount of paid time learning from leading mentor teachers and all teachers collaborate on developing lessons. Lengthening the school day without using time wisely is a recipe for low quality. Darling-Hammond also points out that top-scoring nations have fully supported teacher certification and advanced degrees and that studies in North Carolina and in New York City find overwhelming evidence that teacher quality rises with certification, at least two years of experience, and a strong academic background. All of these professional enhancements make an enormous difference in student achievement that is greater than the effects of race and parental education combined. Her book also contends that top-scoring nations incorporate technology into collaborative learning strategies that give both teachers and students greater freedom for investigation, fostering curiosity, critical thinking, and learning about how to learn. These nations do not replace quality teachers with machines or online education. Last, she reminds readers that top-scoring nations have unionized tenured teachers who are treated as partners in improving quality rather than as adversaries. Studies show that pay for performance schemes are unreliable and methodologically flawed while they also overemphasize test scores, narrow the curriculum, and come at the cost of critical thinking.[27] By making teaching work precarious and insecure, it will be harder for schools to attract and mentor top teachers, and it will also result in high turnover, which will reduce the ranks of experienced teachers. Tenure and seniority, when paired with certification and strong academic preparation, are proven crucial elements of teacher excellence for Darling-Hammond.

Although Darling-Hammond's work presents a challenge to the assumptions animating the *Tribune* editorial board, the broader mass media onslaught, and the rightist assault on unions and teachers across numerous states, like Ravitch's work it fails to address the intersections of cultural politics and political economy. Darling-Hammond emphasizes process and professionalization, but the only way that teacher excellence can ultimately be confirmed is through standardized test scores—rather than, for example, community transformation resulting from critical pedagogical projects, the development of politically engaged intellectual community, and social movements. "Teacher excellence" can ultimately only be affirmed by standardized test scores, and the black boxes of the "strong curriculum" and "student achievement" cannot be questioned for what exactly is being taught and why and how it relates to the purposes and mission of public schools and their role in producing critical agents capable of the kinds of democratic transformation highlighted by Giroux. Both Darling-Hammond and Ravitch call for getting beyond the "curriculum wars" so that educators can accept an allegedly neutral curriculum designed by experts who are somehow magically outside of power and politics. As the presumed goal of public schooling is inclusion into the existing corporate-dominated economy and affirmation of a profoundly exclusionary and purchased electoral democracy, what is taught and what teachers do has nothing to do with challenging the existing unjust configuration of social power.

Ravitch and Darling-Hammond leave untouched some of the most vexing dimensions of corporate school reform. These point to much deeper structural problems that liberals do not want to question and to class and cultural struggles that liberals and many activist-oriented leftists most often evade. These are problems and struggles that are inextricably bound up with the intersection of cultural politics and political economy. This intersection is what Henry Giroux has always taken on squarely and consistently. Most crucially, Giroux's work always links struggles over education to broader class and cultural struggles.[28]

His work calls into question how the forms that knowledge takes relate to expressions of authority. Giroux's emphasis on the necessity of students learning to theorize their experiences and social contexts and to learn new language to interpret, describe, and recast individual and social realities is not an abstract or impractical imperative. On the contrary, in order for students to have the tools to analyze the public pedagogies largely produced by corporate mass media—the most powerful pedagogical apparatus today—theory is a practical necessity for engaged public life. It is not a coincidence that the accommodationist perspectives shared by liberals and conservatives eschew theory as a threat to the efficacious "delivery" of "content knowledge" using the "best methods."

Ravitch, Darling-Hammond, and the majority of liberal reform-oriented education authors criticize standardized testing, because it is "excessive," it "narrows the curriculum," or it is wrongly used to continue funding disparities. In this view, testing is a primarily technical question that interferes with efficient delivery of politically neutral school process. Giroux's early work brought the insights of the Frankfurt School of Critical Theory[29] together with those of Paulo Freire to emphasize how standardized testing and the standardization of curriculum are rather thoroughly political endeavors that deny the politics of the framing and selection of knowledge, thereby obscuring underlying assumptions, values, and ideologies informing such framing and selection of knowledge. The failure of both liberals, left activists, and economistic Marxists to deal adequately with cultural politics leaves them with an inability to address contestations over curriculum and the relationship between claims to truth and the interests and values animating them.

When liberals such as Darling-Hammond deny the politics of the curriculum, such denials often lead to egregious political positions. For example, in her most recent book, Darling-Hammond assumes that America is an empire that needs to be maintained, warning readers that "we don't want to fall like Rome," and she accepts the neoliberal framing of public schooling as principally serving the end of global economic competition. Here we find that one of the leading liberal policy thinkers wraps her liberal calls for equalized educational resources, investment in teacher work, and desegregation in a set of rightist assumptions: education is for competition in a corporate-dominated capitalist economy; the goal of schools is to include more students in the existing social order, not to produce critical citizens who can challenge and transform that order; and what goes on in schools has nothing to do with the political and ethical values behind the maintenance of an imperial military complex. We should remember that Darling-Hammond names her book (*The Flat World and Education*) after Friedman's book *The World Is Flat* and endorses his neoliberal view of a corporately managed planet that requires U.S. military machinery to enforce that order (Friedman: "You can't have McDonald's without McDonnell-Douglas and the military force of the F-15").[30]

Unlike Darling-Hammond, Giroux speaks of the need to reconstruct schooling and pedagogy for global citizenship and global democracy:

> Citizens for a global democracy need to be aware of the interrelated nature of all aspects of physical, spiritual, and cultural life. This means having a deep-rooted understanding of the relational nature of global dependencies, whether we are talking about the ecosphere or the circuits of capital.... Citizens need to cultivate loyalties that extend beyond the nation-state, beyond a theoretical distinction in which the division between friend and enemy is mediated exclusively around national boundaries. Clearly, citizenship as a form of empowerment means acquiring the skills that enable one to critically examine history and resuscitate those dangerous memories in which knowledge expands the possibilities for both self-knowledge and critical and social agency. Knowledge cannot be only indigenous to be empowering.[31]

Many liberals, including Darling-Hammond, think that they can win over neoliberals and other fiscal conservatives by wrapping their liberal demands in neoliberal assumptions such as appeals to economic competition. However, they should consider that the neoliberal think-tank fellows are not interested in redistributing educational resources under any circumstances. If more money is to be invested in education, it should be invested at the top, not the bottom. These liberal appeals fail to comprehend a society constituted by class and cultural conflict. This is a view consistently recognized by Giroux, who emphasizes the extent to which the temporary winning of hegemony requires ongoing pedagogical work. Moreover, Darling-Hammond's liberal appeal to neoliberal values presumes the ethically indefensible position that there have to be global economic winners and losers, and better that the losers make our cell phones and clothes in sweatshops than vice versa. The endlessly repeated mantra of the venture philanthropists and liberal policy wonks that the aim of education is jobs and higher education has nothing to say, as Giroux has pointed out, about unemployment. Nor does it address that changing public priorities such as the funding of education, the expansion of public and caregiving provisions, and the creation of jobs requires social movements and other forms of public engagement. As Giroux's work tirelessly points out, public schools are crucial sites for making engaged critical citizens with the intellectual tools and political agency for the kind of collective public action that is a prerequisite for genuine democracy.

Giroux's work on conceptualizing both the teacher as transformative intellectual and the student as critical citizen are part of the aim for expanding democratic social relations throughout institutions of society. Giroux has been one of a small number of scholars to take on the expanding nexus between the corporatization of education and the rise of an authoritarian culture of militarism in the United States. He has emphasized that a commitment to expanding democracy requires combating all forms of authoritarianism and fundamentalism, and his work insists on the crucial necessity to recognize the pedagogical dimension of educative institutions, including schools and mass media, as well as the pedagogical and political possibilities of individuals and collectivities in producing knowledge. Building on Gramsci, Giroux emphasizes that the pedagogical is always political and the political is always pedagogical. In this context, losing public schools to corporate control results in public schools being captured as one more site for corporate knowledge production and the expansion of consumerism and antidemocratic Social Darwinian forms of sociality. As well, it suggests that the political struggle over the future of public schools is itself a pedagogical project with implicit values that extend to other social struggles.

The liberal positions that depoliticize education and culture, exemplified by Darling-Hammond and postconversion Ravitch, prove utterly inadequate in addressing not only a broader set of life-or-death public problems and the need to produce critical, contemplative, and engaged public citizens, but more specifically the aggressive corporatization agenda. As with corporate advertising-driven media, corporate educational management companies, corporate curricula, and corporate management schemes tend to be hierarchically organized and inevitably have an institutional imperative to frame knowledge and issues in ways that are ideologically compatible with the material interests of the owners. Public schools are contested sites for values and knowledge and as such remain open to the critical pedagogies Giroux's work exemplifies. Privatized schools, often with prepackaged and conservative curriculum and instrumental top-down pedagogies, are foreclosed as sites of political and pedagogical struggle. By reducing schooling to efficacy, reifying knowledge, and affirming the value of standardization and standardized testing, these liberals abandon public schools as contested public spheres—and consequently are stuck in a numbers game with the political right in which the only response to the neoliberal demands is to claim that test-based educational quality can be improved if only enough investment and methodological corrections are made. In this view, knowledge and truth are disconnected from interests, ideologies, subject formation, and broader struggles. These assumptions position public schools of the professional class as beyond question and as a normative benchmark to which poor public schools ought to aspire.

While there is much that is admirable in the public schools that receive heavy investment and that serve professional-class predominantly white citizens, in reality these schools are most often impoverished by their omnipresent but denied political agenda. Their indefensible self-congratulatory ethical posture that class and culturally specific knowledge is neutral and universal fails to take up public problems, human oppression, and the way the society really works systematically to produce vast privilege and market-based forms of agency for some and dire poverty, ecological devastation, and political exclusion for most. The calls of Richard Kahlenberg and Richard Rothstein for expanding "middle class" schools and class-integrated schooling nonetheless do not engage with what exactly is being produced and universalized as "excellence." That is, the norm of the elite professional-class school celebrated by liberals lacks a critical pedagogical approach that links claims to truth to broader structures of power, ideology, subjectivity formation, and political agency best worked out by Giroux.

Liberals and conservatives such as Darling-Hammond and Ravitch call for critical thinking as problem-solving skills, but they reject critical pedagogy's centralizing of power, politics, and ethics as being always linked to pedagogy and demanding ongoing theoretical engagement. The implications of this are particularly glaring when liberals and conservatives accept the concept of the "achievement gap," in which the knowledge and ideologies deemed valuable by the most powerful classes and cultural groups is universalized, and those having socially devalued knowledge and partial knowledge as measured against this norm are stigmatized. In this case, class and cultural difference are positioned as an obstacle to "real learning," measured by the tests. Instead, class and cultural difference ought to form the basis for learning that, as Giroux suggests, is meaningful, that can then be made critical, and that can be the basis for individual and social transformation.[32] Giroux's oeuvre suggests that, in the tradition of Dewey and Freire, public schools can be sites for the ongoing reconstruction of the society—the further democratizing of the political system, the economy, and the culture. The liberal approach stops with the ideal of accommodating students into the existing radically unjust society. Consequently, it has no way of engaging the hostile corporate takeover of public educative institutions and the dire public implications that these carry.

CHAPTER FIVE

TOWARD A NEW COMMON SCHOOL MOVEMENT

RECONCEPTUALIZING EDUCATION FOR SOCIAL JUSTICE GLOBALLY

The prior chapters have made the case that corporate school reform has failed on both its own terms and in terms of public and critical values. Chapter 4 showed how the liberal response to corporate school reform, typified by Ravitch and Darling-Hammond, as well offers an inadequate response to it, eliding both cultural politics and crucial questions of the global economic and political vision for public education. This chapter makes the case for critical educators to develop a new common school movement. It suggests that the alternative to corporate school reform ought, on the one hand, to recover the origins of public schooling in the common school movement and make central the critical education traditions of Dewey, Counts, the reconstructionists, and the critical pedagogy of such thinkers as Paulo Freire, Henry Giroux, and Stanley Aronowitz. On the other hand, an alternative to corporate school reform ought to complement such a recovery of the critical and progressive education traditions for public democratic education by drawing on recent literature on the commons in the humanities and social sciences. This latter addition is the focus of this chapter.

I will begin by briefly considering the relationship of educational privatization to three conceptions of education for social justice. The first is the neoliberal (or market fundamentalist) conception of education for social justice that is dominant and expanding today and that is at the core of corporate school reform.

(While proponents of neoliberal education have hijacked the language of social justice, in reality it is antithetical to social justice, in part because it empties out the very notion of the social from public discourse.)[1] The second is a liberal enlightenment conception of education for social justice, dominant prior to the ascendancy of neoliberal ideology and sought by liberals and many progressives as preferable to corporate school reform.[2] The third is a critical theoretical/critical pedagogical conception of education for social justice. In mapping these three visions of education for social justice, I highlight several ways that the expanding trend toward educational privatization at the center of corporate school reform largely undermines collective public aspirations for emancipation, equality, and the countering of violence and oppression. After mapping these three visions for education, I will suggest that the critical perspective develops and promotes a new critical common school movement to combat neoliberal education and that can contribute to expanding public democratic education for social justice. Before this, though, a few caveats are in order.

First, to talk about education for social justice—as if education can on its own be relied upon to guarantee social justice—is an all too common fallacy characteristic of both the neoliberal and liberal discourses. Putting the onus of social justice on education tends to function as a way of redistributing responsibility for structural conditions and forces from those social actors with the most power to change them to the most local social units (the family and the individual), which, in fact, have the least power over the control and distribution of social resources including education. In the current context, the tendency to treat education apart from other conditions for social justice lends itself particularly to the neoliberal argument for privatization in which the sole aim is greater efficacy of delivery of allegedly neutral educational services. In this view, educational privatization is framed as a tool (proven or not) for effecting the end of increased quantity and quality and decreased cost. A related caveat involves the limitations of comprehending the content of education (curriculum, pedagogy, administration, and so on) as neutral or apolitical. Although the aspirations for social justice ought to be comprehended as universal (cessation of oppression, ending violence and all forms of exploitation, collective aspirations for equality and emancipation, democratic control over social institutions), educational institutions are sites of struggle by competing groups. Any attempt at fostering social justice in schools has to contend with the local context and power relations as well as the ways broader structural forces inform the context. In other words, questions of educational privatization need to be understood in terms not just of political economy (questions of ownership, control, governance, funding, and distribution) but also of the cultural politics of education (questions of the unequal exchanges of meanings, the politics of knowledge production). I contend here that the political economic questions of educational privatization impact the cultural politics of education.

Three Visions of Education for Social Justice

Neoliberal Privatization and Social Justice

Globally in the past thirty years, it has become impossible to understand public school privatization initiatives apart from the dominant ideological trend of neoliberalism. Neoliberalism, a form of radical fiscal conservatism, alternately described as "neoclassical economics" and "market fundamentalism," originates with Frederic Von Hayek, Milton Friedman, and the "Chicago boys" at the University of Chicago in the 1950s. Within this view, individual and social ideals can best be achieved through the "unfettered market." In its ideal forms (as opposed to how it is practically implemented), neoliberalism calls for privatization of public goods and services, decreased regulation of trade, loosening of capital and labor controls by the state, and the allowance of foreign direct investment. In the view of neoliberalism, public control over public resources should be shifted out of the hands of the necessarily bureaucratic state and into the hands of the necessarily efficient private sector.

In industrialized nations, educational privatization takes the form of for-profit management of schools, "performance contracting," for-profit and nonprofit charter schools, school vouchers, school commercialism, for-profit online education, online homeschooling, test publishing and textbook industries, electronic and computer-based software curriculum, for-profit remediation, and educational contracting, to name but a partial list. The modeling of public schooling on business runs from classroom pedagogy that replicates corporate culture to the contracting out of management of districts, the corporatization of the curriculum, and the "partnerships" that schools form with the business "community" that aim to market to kids.

In developing nations, fee-based for-profit schooling is being increasingly seized upon by neoliberal institutions like the World Bank/International Monetary Fund, World Economic Forum, and World Trade Organization, and academics such as James Tooley (darling of the World Bank), who aim to elaborate on how for-profit schooling is both superior in quality and ethically driven, unlike public schooling. Tooley's arguments (in his book *The Beautiful Tree*, for example, published by neoliberal think tank CATO) rely heavily on anecdotal bashing of public schooling, anecdotal celebration of low-fee private schooling, and a number of unsubstantiated and contradictory neoliberal assumptions. Most centrally, he touts the claim that what makes the private schools superior is the market incentives for educational entrepreneurs to start schools—incentives that are lacking in public schooling. But then he claims that not solely incentives, but rather status and the desire of these entrepreneurs to do social work as philanthropists explain their motives. Tooley spends much of his book celebrating the successes of low-fee for-profit schools only to conclude by calling for foreign capital to build franchises of for-profits to compete against these schools (McDonalds is the model). He advises that public money should be put into branding and advertising because of the virtues of standardization of schools and their brands, and that private philanthropic money should go not to support public schooling but to support forms of schooling for which profit can be drained out for investors. The basis of Tooley's romantic picture of privatization is the existing local private "low fee" school, which he first uses to justify radical expansion of privatization. His concludes by calling for foreign direct investment so that the schools in poor nations can be transformed on the model of the fast food industry (I'm not making this up!). Tooley fails to deal with the fact that educational development modeled on the fast food industry would utterly transform both the local low-fee schools that he celebrates and the alleged status-based incentives for running private schools that he supports and that justify his argument. Tooley calls for ending public education, not for strengthening it or developing it where it is absent. The postscript reveals Tooley to have accepted a job as a manager of a $100 million education investment fund.[3]

Tooley's view coincides with those of the three Bs: rock star Bono, Bill Gates, and Bill Clinton, who preach a new "gospel of wealth" in which the only way to do good is for the super-rich to do well. In their view, educational access can only be achieved by creating the conditions for investor profit. Their views differ, however, from the original liberal "Gospel of Wealth" promoted by Andrew Carnegie, who called on the rich to give to support public knowledge-making institutions like libraries, museums, and schools so that the individual could have the opportunity for self-improvement through free access to information. The three Bs promote the privatization of access to information, with Gates having made the largest fortune on the planet through commercializing the freely exchanged software in the hippy tech movement of the 1970s and pushing educational privatization through venture philanthropy, Bono trying to fight free exchange of music and cultural production as he and his U2 bandmates squirrel away their millions in tax avoidance schemes in the Netherlands, and Bill Clinton's neoliberal postpolitical denial of the ideology and politics that characterized his presidency and his private-sector approach to philanthropy that dominates his Clinton Global Initiative. Although neoliberalism denies politics, as David Harvey emphasizes, it should be understood as a tool of class warfare waged by the rich on the rest. The prominence of the three Bs suggests that study of educational privatization has to comprehend the role of mass media, publicity, and public relations in shaping educational reform debates globally and the relationships between these forms of publicity and broader ideological trends and movements.

Neoliberalism appears in the now commonsense framing of education exclusively through presumed ideals of upward individual economic mobility (the promise of cashing in knowledge for jobs) and the social ideals of global economic competition. Margaret Thatcher's TINA thesis (There Is No Alternative), which has come to dominate politics throughout much of the world, has infected educational thought. The only questions on neoliberal educational reform agendas appear to be how to enforce knowledge and curriculum conducive to national economic interest and the expansion of a corporately managed model of globalization as perceived from the perspective of business. Education in this view is seen as ideally accommodating the student to the existing social order. Framed out within this view are the role of democratic participation in societies ideally committed to democracy and the role of public schools in preparing public democratic citizens with the tools for meaningful and participatory self-governance. Also framed out is the pursuit of global justice in forms that break with neoliberal globalization, such as the global justice movement and other grassroots movements for justice.

By reducing the politics and ethics of education largely to its economic roles, neoliberal educational reform has deeply authoritarian tendencies that are incompatible with democratic social relations, popular power, and the intellectual tools for social criticism as the basis for just social change. The authoritarian tendencies of neoliberal educational reform owe themselves in part to the modeling of the school and school reform on the corporation, a decidedly hierarchical institution organized by authoritarian rather than egalitarian relations. These tendencies also are the product of the neoliberal ethical egoist vision of the individual as motivated by selfishness or self-interest and a vision of the social understood through Social Darwinist competition. There is little place in this view to comprehend the ways that individual ethical choices are informed by institutional contexts. Nor is there much sense of the historical struggles for justice that have been waged by individuals and groups to create better living and working conditions. These struggles resulted not from the ethos of competitive individualism characteristic of neoliberalism but rather out of ethical convictions, often radical critiques of existing institutions and practices and the imagination of radically different alternatives to the present.

Globally, a neoliberal declaration of public system failure undergirds the claims for radical market-based restructuring, as does the description of public service as privately deliverable. These framings are important for how they shift educational provision to the private field of business competition, framing out the public dimensions of schooling, including civic and ethical dimensions.

For neoliberalism, the social, public, humanistic possibilities of education are subordinated to the primary goal of efficient delivery. Privatization in the neoliberal view is linked to the historical legacy of positivist rationality[4] with its tendency to treat knowledge in a static, neutral way. Positivism presumes that knowledge can be collected, measured, quantified, standardized, and delivered. The linkage of privatization with positivist rationality allows for knowledge to be treated as units of commodity (this has been a boon for educational markets in the testing and test publishing, tutoring, and contracting markets), but it also naturalizes a chain of economically defined promotions: the student consumes the right knowledge that has been determined in advance by experts; the student is tested and rewarded or punished for consuming this knowledge; and the student is promoted to higher levels of schooling to the end point of exchanging these educational honors for inclusion in the corporate-dominated economy, where he or she can fully express his or her life as a consumer or worker. Cultural conservatism (typified by E. D. Hirsch, Diane Ravitch, and the Common Core curriculum trend) with its dogmatic view of knowledge has a natural affinity with this positivism, as canonized claims to truth can be more easily standardized, tested, and mass marketed. The business model appears in schools in the push for standardization and routinization with emphases on standardization of curriculum, standardized testing, methods-based instruction, teacher deskilling, scripted lessons, and a number of approaches aiming for "efficient delivery" of instruction. The business model presumes that teaching, like factory production, can be evermore speeded up and made more efficient through technical modifications to instruction and incentives for teachers and students, like cash bonuses. Holistic, critical, and socially oriented approaches to learning that understand pedagogical questions in relation to power are eschewed as privatization and corporatization instrumentalize knowledge, disconnecting knowledge from the broader political, ethical, and cultural struggles informing interpretations and claims to truth while denying differential material power to make meanings.

With the financial crisis of 2008, the neoliberal dictates of unfettered deregulation and privatization have become discredited by numerous economists. Nonetheless, continuing unabated, the neoliberal perspective imagines public education as a private market that will necessarily benefit from competition and choice, privatization and deregulation. Knowledge and schooling are increasingly being framed by global organizations as responsible to save capitalism. At the same time, the neoliberal vision for education fosters an abdication of the social altogether as education is positioned as the means for individuals to negotiate what Bauman calls "the individualized society."[5]

Liberal Conception of Education for Social Justice

The enlightenment liberal philosophical tradition emphasizes the role of education in making the autonomous individual and preparing the citizen for political participation in the existing political system proper. Education appears as a means of individual humanistic edification and the basis for individual upward economic mobility. Within the liberal tradition, education facilitates the accommodation of the individual to the existing economic and political order. The liberal tradition tends to approach schooling, knowledge, and curriculum as the pursuit of universal truth and the accumulation of neutral knowledge. Power struggles over claims to truth and their relationship to the claimants are not a part of the liberal view. Consequently, education is perceived as a largely apolitical endeavor. The crucial issue becomes the effective transmission of an accumulated body of knowledge through "good schooling," which can be measured through "student achievement." Although liberal approaches to schooling vary in their embrace of the equation of student achievement with testing, the claim to universal value and neutrality of knowledge results in a conception of knowledge as somewhat static, inheritable, and transmissible. Hence, the perspective on educational privatization tends to focus on efficacy of delivery. Privatization initiatives are most often viewed as a potential tool or threat to increasing effective delivery.

Linda Darling-Hammond, perhaps the most influential liberal educational policy scholar, typifies this position by calling for a depoliticized view of the content of schooling by declaring the need for an end to the "destructive curriculum wars" (that is, rejecting a political understanding of how it is that what schools do relates to broader interests and struggles) and then calling for a focus on access to "expert teachers," "high-quality curriculum opportunities," "good educational materials," and so on.[6] Darling-Hammond and other liberals want to view the curriculum and pedagogical approaches as outside of politics, yet when it comes to defining what is meant by "expert," "good," or "high quality," political values are, of course, smuggled back in. In Darling-Hammond's case the project for liberal educational inclusion and access is toward the end of a neoliberal vision of national economy and global economic competition and making sure that the American Empire doesn't fall the way Rome did.[7]

The liberal tradition tends to affirm structures of power as unquestionable (capitalism paired with a liberal parliamentary form of electoral democracy) and seeks to utilize education as a means to greater assimilation. Social justice in this view is dominated by the logic of educational inclusion and the ideal of ameliorating or tweaking existing systems to make them more inclusive. If only more citizens can be educated, then they can be included into the economy, the political system, and the dominant culture. Unlike neoliberalism, the liberal tradition tends to value the public sector. Educational privatization, contracting, and market-based experiments largely appear within these assumptions as potential tools to further public ends. Liberals tend to be skeptical of aspects of privatization, such as school commercialism, for tainting the otherwise allegedly neutral space of learning. They tend to be skeptical of privatization initiatives that drain public resources from the public system. They are also leery of neoliberal privatization efforts to remove teachers' unions and crush local governance in the form of school boards. Yet, the issue of efficacy of delivery trumps all.

The liberal view tends to assume that equality is defined by equality of opportunity. What they call "equal opportunity" is ultimately the responsibility of the individual who can use freely available knowledge to better the self by competing on a largely level playing field. If the playing field is not exactly level, then it can always be leveled a little through tinkering. However, as Stanley Aronowitz writes, criticizing the liberal dimensions of Deweyan pragmatism, equality of opportunity presumes class inequality as a social norm. Aronowitz and other advocates of critical approaches to education contend that inequality should not be presumed as a social baseline and that education should be about creating the conditions for radically democratic social relations with regard to politics, culture, and economics.[8] Aronowitz's point is that the rhetoric of "access to opportunity" has resulted in naturalizing a durably unequal social order. Educational "access to opportunity" has become evermore emphasized in political rhetoric as, in reality, class mobility has significantly declined in the past several decades. It is the responsibility of teachers, schools, administrators, and parents to magically counter the upward redistribution of wealth and radically worsened income inequality by teaching better? More efficient teaching methods are going to provide an antidote to class exploitation or the logic of capital or to radical inequalities in wealth and income or to massive child poverty rates? Though many liberals do see the use of public state power to ameliorate numerous social ills, they tend to lack an understanding of how cultural symbolic hierarchies are intertwined with material inequalities.[9]

From a liberal and critical perspective, the privatization of public schools and the ideology of corporate culture need to be opposed. For liberals, the goal is to strengthen public schools. The various forms of privatization undermine the liberal promises of public schooling to make educated human beings and a thoughtful participating polity. From a liberal perspective, even though historically the public sector has failed to provide universal quality educational services equally to everyone, that still remains the goal. In this view, the expansion of the "best" schools—that is, those schools from class, culturally, and racially privileged areas—remains the model. U.S. liberals such as Jonathan Kozol highlight the spending disparities between the rich predominantly white schools and the poor predominantly African American and Latino schools. Per pupil, rich schools get as much as four times more money than poor schools, while poor schools actually need more than rich schools.[10] For liberals, the project of educational equality is very much defined by the equalization of educational resources toward the goal of inclusion—the equalization of educational opportunity is supposed to translate into economic and political opportunity for participation in existing institutions. For liberals, privatization threatens to skim out of the system as investor profit resources. Such resources for liberals could be better reinvested in public provision toward the end of extending the excellence of elite public schools to all.

The liberal perspective does not just evade deep structural class inequality and its reproduction but also contributes to the simultaneous production and denial of symbolic hierarchies. One of the most glaring examples of this is what we might term the "poverty of suburban schooling." Suburban, professional class, largely white schools are represented in liberal discourse as the ideal toward which working-class and nonwhite schools ought to aspire. Meanwhile, these idealized schools foist on students a profoundly ideological curriculum and pedagogy that is universally acclaimed to be both excellent and politically neutral. The idealization of the knowledge of the privileged rather than its critical interrogation is typified in the idea of the "achievement gap" in which the knowledge norms of the privileged are held up as the ideal. In the achievement gap framing, non-privileged groups are disparaged for failing to take in and then display mastery of knowledge that has been falsely deemed universally valuable, politically neutral, and outside of critical scrutiny. This framing denies the cultural politics of the curriculum while concealing the elevation of particular knowledge, values, and tastes of privileged groups into the norm.

Educational Privatization and Social Justice from a Critical Perspective

For criticalists, the defense of public schools against neoliberal privatization is about defending the public sector with the goal of critical transformation of the political and economic systems via the political and cultural struggle waged through civil society. In this sense, the cultural struggle to make public schools sites for the making of critical consciousness is crucial and is distinct from the liberal perspective. From a critical perspective, schools can be democratic public spheres that can foster critical consciousness, democratic dispositions, and habits of engaged citizenry. From a critical perspective, schools play a crucial role in producing subject positions, identifications, and social relations that can make radically democratic subjects committed to such projects as democratizing the economy, strengthening the public roles of the state, challenging oppressive institutions and practices, and participating in democratic culture. As well, from a critical perspective, knowledge is subject to interrogation in relation to power, questions of politics, history, and ethics. Experience needs to be problematized and theorized in relation to broader social, cultural, and political struggles, forces, and realities informing experience. Such critical examination of subjective experience in relation to objective forces ideally in the critical perspective becomes the basis for agency and action directed at transforming oppressive forces and structures.

Liberal and conservative perspectives on public schooling operate through accommodationism. That is, they presume that we live in a fundamentally just social order and that the role of public schools is to accommodate students to that order.

Although historically and presently, state-administered public schooling functions hegemonically, both privatization and the ideology of corporate culture deepen the conservatizing tendencies of public schooling rather than unsettle them. As Nancy Fraser emphasizes,[11] the shift to a neoliberal post-Fordist economic and social configuration burst open the national frame, fostering an increasingly dual society of self-regulating entrepreneurial subjects for professional-class people and repression for the excluded working class and poor.

> Finally, as fordist discipline wanes in the face of globalization, its orientation to self-regulation tends to dissipate too. As more of the work of socialization is marketized, fordism's labor-intensive individualizing focus tends to drop out. In psychotherapy, for example, the time-intensive talk-oriented approaches favored under fordism are increasingly excluded from insurance coverage and replaced by instant-fix pharma-psychology. In addition, the enfeeblement of Keynesian state steering means more unemployment and less downward redistribution, hence increased inequality and social instability. The resulting vacuum is more likely to be filled by outright repression than by efforts to promote individual autonomy. In the U.S., accordingly some observers posit the transformation of the social state into a "prison-industrial complex," where incarceration of male minority youth becomes the favored policy on unemployment. The prisons in question, moreover, have little in common with the humanist panopticons described by Foucault. Their management often subcontracted to for-profit corporations, they are less laboratories of self-reflection than hotbeds of racialized and sexualized violence—of rape, exploitation, corruption, untreated HIV, murderous gangs, and murderous guards. If such prisons epitomize one aspect of postfordism, it is one that no longer works through individual self-governance. Here, rather we encounter the return of repression, if not the return of the repressed.[12]

Privatization is increasingly linked to repression as for-profit prisons and schools become less about rehabilitation and self-improvement and more about warehousing, containment, and repressive control. Just as prisons are racialized hotbeds of repression, the privatization of schools fosters a similar logic. In predominantly working-class and poor schools populated by students of color, scripted lessons for teachers sold by educational contractors are joined with rigid bodily control for students designed and implemented by private management companies. Such repression is justified on the alleged best interests of poor students of color, who need to submit to such discipline if they are to have an opportunity to reap the rewards of the capitalist economy. As the United States continues massive upward redistributions of wealth, income inequality, the decimation of organized labor, and downward mobility, the "opportunity" of "cashing in" on submission to a rigged game appears to countless students as ludicrous. Poor students of color witness economic survival composed of working three minimum-wage jobs without benefits for the lucky ones. Within both the liberal and conservative views accommodation to the existing economic order through education (as difficult or impossible as it may be for masses of students) is built on an assumption that the global economy is a zero-sum game with necessary losers making the cell phones and appliances of the winners. That is, in the West, the role of education for the neoliberal dream of ever-greater economic growth is premised on the pursuit of cheap exploited labor in poor nations and a global race to the bottom.

In the 1990s and 2000s, liberals and progressives who considered the corporatization of schools largely responded to an economic framing of public education with a political framing of it. Corporate school reformers have argued that the schools ought to prepare individuals for inclusion in the corporate economy by creating workers and consumers who could contribute to global economic competition. In response, liberals and progressives have insisted on the traditional political role of public schools in creating engaged citizens who can participate in public life and self-governance. They have insisted that corporatizing schools transforms the mission and purpose of schooling, gutting its public and civic roles, privatizing and individualizing it. Such criticisms are correct. But they are also limited in that they have not adequately dealt with the intertwined political, economic, and cultural dimensions of the corporatization agenda. Most liberals and progressives have assumed that public schooling should prepare students for existing capitalism in addition to preparing them as citizens. And the corporate school reformers have joined the game, adding "citizenship" to the primarily economic framing of public schooling. However, while critical education has always presumed that schooling should be the basis for transforming society and its institutions, it has remained relatively quiet on the role of public schools in transforming the economy.[13] If public schooling is to foster a more democratic vision of the economy than that of the corporate school reformers, then where to look?

Toward a New Common School Movement

In what follows, I draw on recent scholarship on "the commons" and suggest that we need to appropriate selectively from some of its key contributors while rejecting certain aspects by some contributors in order to imagine a new common school movement. I then suggest some insights that such work on the commons has for critical education's contribution to social renewal. The matter at hand here is not developing a better form of school reform than corporate school reform, because neither schooling nor broader social structures can be simply reformed. What is at stake in imagining a new common school is dauntingly enormous and radically hopeful—the possibility of imagining a new form of collective living, working, and consuming.

The Original Common School Movement

The U.S. public school system has its origins in the common school movement spearheaded first in Massachusetts by Horace Mann in the early nineteenth century. The movement eventually spread throughout the United States. Mann emphasized the need for an educated public in a functioning democracy, a system of publicly financed schools, that schools should be composed of children of different backgrounds, that education should be nonsectarian, that students should be taught by professionally trained teachers, and that the educational disciplines and methods should express the values of a free society. The common school movement was promoted as a means of political inclusion, workforce preparation, and individual character building aiming to bring together children of different classes and provide a common learning experience. The common school movement sought to increase provision of educational resources, including the quality of schools, increased duration of schooling to the age of sixteen, better pay for the mostly female teacher workforce, and a broader curriculum.

Many aspects of public schooling have been struggled over since the common school movement began—including racial segregation and integration, the question of secular versus religious-based moral instruction, the politics of the curriculum, and the role of public schools in workforce preparation. The neoliberal privatization that began to take hold in the 1990s has in many respects undone many socially valuable aspects of the legacy of the common school movement. Aspirations of a common educational experience, the commitment to nonsectarian schooling, and the value of educated citizenry for public participation are collateral damage in the privatization trend. Voucher schemes, homeschooling, and scholarship tax credits have contributed to an effort, especially embraced by the Christian right, to capture public resources to pay for religious education.

The neoliberal emphasis on schooling for work and consumption has dramatically undermined the central value of promoting democratic citizens imbued with the knowledge and disposition for self-governance. The relentless push for charter schooling has resegregated public schools. Magnets were transformed as well during President Ronald Reagan's administration from being an effort in racial integration and equity into being seen as a "market" in schools. The values on universal and equal provision and the common benefit to publicly paying for schooling has been damaged severely by the centrality of the metaphors of "competition" and consumer "choice." In addition to transforming schooling into something that is more class stratified, neoliberal privatization redefines schooling as an individualized responsibility undermining the sense of shared value for the benefit of others.

Corporate school reform represents hopelessness for the future and an assumption that unlimited capitalist growth is the only alternative. That is, corporate school reform not only actively contributes to the reproduction of economic exploitation, political marginalization, and the crushing of imagination as all social and individual values are reduced to market concerns; it also contributes to planetary destruction, which makes life on the planet a kind of terminal illness as we wait out the imminent cascade of ecological collapse and human disaster in responding to it. As a number of scholars have suggested, capitalism and its imperative for unlimited growth of consumption is a waste production system, not only despoiling the planet but also rendering wasted lives and disposable populations.[14] But as I argued in Chapter 3, corporate school reform installs and extends a culture of control that is at odds with freedom understood as collectively enacted aspirations. As well, as I contend in Chapter 1, the economic promises of corporate school reform are false promises. The promise of corporate school reform toward the end of workforce preparation and university enrollment has no way of dealing with the global race to the bottom for cheap precarious labor. Corporate school reform asks citizens to have faith in corporations for their future economic well-being. Such faith is profoundly misplaced, both because the institutional interests of corporations are (by law) for profit and because gains in labor conditions—such as the end of child labor, the creation of the weekend, the eight-hour work day, and benefits—were the result not of the beneficence of corporations but of social movements. Indeed, as the eighty-cents-an-hour university-educated knowledge workers proofreading academic textbooks in the tax-free zones (maquiladoras) in Jamaica illustrate, a global corporate governance infrastructure that deregulates capital and labor and defunds the public sector creates the conditions for a super-exploited highly educated labor force. Preventing that requires either revitalized labor movement, social democratic state intervention, or, as Richard Wolff has argued, the collectivization of industries such that workers and managers become the same people.[15]

Corporate School Reform Is an Enclosure of the Commons

Corporate school reform is not merely about better or worse school reform approaches—adjusting pedagogical methods, tweaking the curriculum, and so on. It is crucially about redistributed control over social life and as such is part of a much broader trend. It represents a capitalist enclosure of the commons—that is, the violent taking of "the shared substance of our social being."[16] As Slavoj Zizek points out, there are three crucial enclosures of the commons at present:

- *the commons of culture*, the immediately socialized forms of "cognitive capital," primarily language, our means of communication and education, but also the shared infrastructure of public transport, electricity, the postal system, and so on;
- *the commons of external nature*, threatened by pollution and exploitation (from oil to rain forests and the natural habitat itself);
- *the commons of internal nature* (the biogenetic inheritance of humanity); with new biogenetic technology, the creation of a New Man (sic.) in the literal sense of changing human nature becomes a realistic prospect.[17]

A fourth enclosure of the common involves the de facto apartheid situation of new "walls and slums" that physically enclose people, separating the Excluded from the Included. These four enclosures of the common are being struggled over and the stakes in the struggle are, for Zizek, the very survival of the species and the planet itself. Capitalist enclosure of the natural commons produces ecological catastrophe. Capitalist enclosure of the knowledge commons makes ideas into private property rather than freely shared and exchanged knowledge of use and potential universal benefit. Capitalist enclosure transforms the biological information that is the stuff of life into property, setting the stage for new forms of bio-slavery and profit-based control. Corporate school reform colludes with and deepens these enclosures of the commons. It makes knowledge into a commodity rather than being shared and freely exchanged. It naturalizes a natural world defined by private ownership rather than public care. It privatizes the process of maturation and socialization, making human development into business and children into product. Finally, the lower tier of privatized public schooling expands repression in the form of new walls and slums.

The most significant aspect of corporate school reform involves privatizing the public schools. In an economic sense, privatization involves enclosing commonly held wealth, assets, and land. Value is produced by collective labor in any enterprise. But capitalism individualizes the profits from collective labor. As David Harvey points out, the common as a form of collective laboring must ground collective rather than individualized property rights and result in collective control over the production process.[18] Public schools are not simply commonly held property, but the collective labor of teachers, administrators, and staff composes the common of the public schools as well. As Harvey explains,

> The collective laboring that is now productive of value must ground collective, not individual, property rights. Value, socially necessary labor time, is the capitalist common, and it is represented by money, the universal equivalency by which common wealth is measured. The common is not, therefore, something extant once upon a time that has since been lost, but something that, like the urban commons, is continuously being produced. The problem is that it is just as continuously being enclosed and appropriated by capital in its commodified and monetary form.[19]

Corporate school reform does just this. It encloses and appropriates for capital the collective *labor* of teachers, administrators, staff, and students. And it does so by using public financing for privatizing public schooling. In fact, as real estate schemes by charters and the vast array of contracting deals exemplify, corporate school reform also encloses the collective *property* of the public school. In some cases the actual public school building is given to a private entity such as a charter school. More frequently, the contracting arrangements that districts make with for-profit firms result in the extraction of surplus wealth, most often by decreasing teacher pay and skimming off profit by contractors. For Harvey, the problem of the commons is that unregulated individualized capital accumulation threatens to destroy the laborer and the land, which are the two basic common property resources. The previous chapters have detailed the extent of these destructions to the common property resources of the public schools. For example, unregulated individualized capital accumulation destroys the teacher (laborer) by transforming her/his work from having the potential for intellectual, civically engaged, dialogic, and fostering of curiosity, questioning, and dissent into anti-intellectual, de-politicized, dogmatic, transmissional, curiosity deadening, and creativity stifling.

Corporate school reform destroys the public and civic dimensions of schooling in addition to the economic productive force of it. Unregulated individualized capital accumulation also destroys the labor of the student and the economic productiveness of the student's future economic labor. The overemphasis on standardized testing and standardization of curriculum devalues the teacher's engagement with the specific context and experience of the student and in doing so makes it impossible for the act of teaching to produce the kind of subject that would engage in collective creative production. Corporate school reform transforms the student's relationship to creative activity and to time.

Proponents of corporate school reform believe that it increases the efficiency of the teacher-laborer through the enforcement of discipline (tighter controls over time, subject matter, and pedagogical methods) and that such efficiency increases the delivery of knowledge to the student-consumer, increasing, in turn, the potential economic efficiency of the future student-worker. This is not so. For example, chartering, which has become captured by a corporate logic that views it as ripe for profit extraction, aims to replicate and scale up the most efficient delivery models, extend the teacher day, pay the teacher less, burn the teacher out, and turn over the teacher workforce. All of these are proven effects of chartering, and there is no doubt that they are good means of maximizing short-term profit for for-profit management companies and other contractors. The problem is not only, as liberals like Darling-Hammond emphasize, that these destructive reforms are bad for test-based student achievement.[20] More significant, these are means of worsening the creative, intellectual, curiosity-fostering, and critically engaged qualities of teaching and also worsening the future productive force of the students' labor.[21] Controlled, rigid, anticritical teaching results not in subjects with a greater capacity for economic productivity but the opposite. If the goal is to produce docile, disciplined low-skill workers or marginalized people who are excluded from the economy altogether, these corporate school reforms are right on target. However, ethics and politics aside, this is shortsighted as an economic strategy if, as the corporate school reformers allege, the aim of public schooling is to produce future high-tech workers with knowledge of math and science who can create new value. The dominant justification for corporate school reform is for the United States to develop its labor capacity in the high-technology arena toward the end of winning global economic competition. Usually, proponents of the dominant justification call for encouraging students to develop their capacities for entrepreneurialism. It is difficult to see how eroding the capacity of teacher labor to inspire vigorous, creative thinking and intellectual curiosity could contribute to such a capitalist goal. The point not to be missed here is that even on its own bad terms of education for capitalist accumulation, corporate school reform undermines its own aims. Enclosure of the public school through privatization does create short-term profit, but it destroys the labor and resources of the public school—that is, it destroys the value of it by pillaging it as productive force. As I have argued and illustrated in *Capitalizing on Disaster*, such pillaging of public services has become a means for the acquisition of short-term profit while destroying long-term value.

Lois Weiner argues that despite the rhetoric of "excellence promotion" accompanying privatization, deregulation, and managerialist policies, corporate school reforms that target working-class and poor students are designed to deskill and deprofessionalize teachers and produce a low-paid, low-skilled future workforce for their students (educated to the eighth grade).[22] Weiner's attention to how this plays out in the documents and practices of global economic organizations such as the World Bank/International Monetary Fund are confirmed in the United States in the form, for example, of the 21st Century Skills initiative as well as the report *Tough Choices for Tough Times*. There is official rhetoric, for example, coming from the Gates Foundation and the U.S. Department of Education that individual economic opportunity will come from increasing high school and graduation rates.[23] Yet, these claims invert the cause-and-effect of education and employment by suggesting that the education level of the individual creates the job opportunity instead of recognizing that the high levels of low-pay, low-skill unemployment are structurally part of the economy.[24] Put differently, we must ask whether high levels of education create employment. Evidence suggests that political maneuvering and economic development activities to lure professional jobs to states and locales is more about stealing jobs from other states and locales than it is about job creation.[25] There is a domestic race to the bottom for jobs in which states compete to see who can offer the best tax breaks to businesses that deplete public coffers while inducing other states to compete by giving up future public revenues. As well, the reliance on education to provide employment opportunities for professional-class people has little to say about the loss of professional jobs to nations with cheaper labor costs but high education levels (legal jobs, accounting jobs, IT jobs, and so on, leaving the United States for India and Singapore are the obvious examples). Without protections, such labor disappears in the global race to the bottom.

Another possibility for education for economic development exists in the form of new kinds of labor and productiveness developing. The neoliberal version of this argument (see Chapter 4) suggests that students need to be made into entrepreneurs so that they can add value to the corporate workplace. In this absurd tale, the unemployment rate would be lower if only employees had learned in school to be more entrepreneurial at work. Capital outlay plays no role in such entrepreneurialism, and the stories that typically are used to justify this explanation for how education automatically creates value include tales of Facebook app creations that net advertising revenue. Such thinking can be found in Darling-Hammond's *The Flat World and Education,* where she affirms Friedman's assumptions by claiming that schools need to be improved because the workers of tomorrow will be doing jobs that do not yet exist. For Friedman, Darling-Hammond, the majority of the educational establishment, and popular discourse, education sets the stage for global economic capitalist competition. In these ways of thinking about education, reform aims toward future *collective labor* to be directed toward *individualized gains.*

Does the Distinction Between Public and Private Matter in Education?

David Harvey concludes his short essay "The Future of Commons" by suggesting that the particulars of institutional arrangements (including public and private) are not important. Rather, what matters is to organize production, distribution, exchange, and consumption to use *collective labor* for *common good.* What is at stake is the question of whether the public/private distinction for schooling matters once the aim is established as collective labor for common good.

> What matters here is not the particular mix of institutional arrangements—enclosures here, extensions of a variety of collective and common property arrangements there—but that the unified effect address the spiraling degradation of common labor and common land resources (including the resources embedded in the "second nature" of the built environment) at the hands of capital. In this effort, the "rich mix of instrumentalities" ... not only public and private but also collective and associational, nested hierarchical and horizontal, exclusionary and open—will all have a key role to play in finding ways to organize production, distribution, exchange, and consumption to meet human needs. The point is not to fulfill the requirements of accumulation for accumulation's sake on the part of the class that appropriates the common wealth from the

class that produces it. The point, rather, is to change all that and to find creative ways to use the powers of collective labor for the common good.[26]

If critical educators accept the values of collective labor for the common good, two crucial questions arise. First, does that mean that the relationship between public and private does not matter for schooling and that, as Harvey suggests, there can be different strategies and instrumentalities toward the end of common labor for the common good? Second, what does a common school *do* to create the social conditions for collective labor for the common good?

In "Ideology and Ideological State Apparatuses," Louis Althusser explains his, Marx's, and Gramsci's views on the irrelevancy of the public/private distinction to the wielding of power through and by the state. Althusser notes that the distinction is internal to bourgeois property law, and so the public already presumes private property relations. The Marxist tradition has little use for retaining the public/private distinction and relegates politics generally to the domain of ideology, a mere reflection of the material base. Althusser offers a richer vision of ideology that is not simply a reflective theory of correspondence, yet he retains the dismissal of the public sphere as an ideological effect.

> The distinction between the public and the private is a distinction internal to bourgeois law, and valid in the (subordinate) domains in which bourgeois law exercises its "authority." The domain of the State escapes it because the latter is "above the law": the State, which is the State of the ruling class, is neither public nor private; on the contrary, it is the precondition for any distinction between public and private. The same thing can be said from the starting point of our State Ideological Apparatuses. It is unimportant whether the institutions in which they are realized are "public" or "private." What matters is how they function. Private institutions can perfectly well "function" as Ideological State Apparatuses. A reasonably thorough analysis of any one of the ISAs proves it.[27]

The state in this tradition is reduced to being an arm of capital. For Althusser, while the repressive state apparatuses—such as the military and the police—function principally through violence, the ideological state apparatuses, including the schools, the media, and the church, function principally through ideology. And Althusser retains the emphasis on the centrality of ideology to the reproduction of capital. The school, for example, creates the student, who not only has the knowledge and skills for the capitalist to exploit her labor but also learns in school the dispositions, tastes, and ways of socially relating such that she submits to the authority of the boss, the hierarchy of the workplace, and so on.

> But it is by an apprenticeship in a variety of know-how wrapped up in the massive inculcation of the ideology of the ruling class that the relations of production in a capitalist social formation, i.e., the relations of exploited to exploiters and exploiters to exploited, are largely reproduced.[28]

For Althusser, the school has become the dominant ideological state apparatus, replacing the church and subjecting its captive audience to ideological subject formation in ways that depoliticize, naturalize, and neutralize the political project of making obedient, exploited, and exploitable workers. Today in the United States, tests and curricular standardization play a central ideological role of accomplishing the denial of class politics.

> The mechanisms which produce this vital result for the capitalist regime are naturally covered up and concealed by a universally reigning ideology of the School, universally reigning because it is one of the essential forms of the ruling bourgeois ideology: an ideology which represents the School as a neutral environment purged of ideology.[29]

Famously, a limitation of Althusser's conception of politics as organized by the ideological subject formation of the Ideological State Apparatus is that it renders an account of power in which the formation of subjects through interpellation happens mechanistically, through the act of hailing. There is little space in this account for how subjects mediate, resist, and fail to be made into "good" subjects. There is also an absent account of the pedagogical production of subjectivity and agency. This is significant in part because any critical pedagogical approach would need to foster critical agency and be attentive to subject formation and how subjects mediate objects of knowledge. Also at stake is the question of how public versus private institutions and agents differently create the conditions for criticality, agency, and mediation.

If we consider corporate school reform in terms of the recent literature on the commons, we can ask the question of how it helps us formulate a response to the problems posed by public school privatization in terms of economic control, political control, and cultural control. Rather than asking whether privatization threatens critical, public, and democratic forms of education, which we assume is a given, the question is: *How do critical forms of education create the conditions for collective labor toward collective benefit, and how do private forms of education create the conditions for collective labor toward private benefit?*

Part of what is at stake in the privatization of schools is the diminishment of the public sphere. We should recognize that there are at least four clear ways that those committed to democratic education must understand how public control differs from private control.

1. **Public versus private ownership and control:** for-profit education companies are able to skim public tax money that would otherwise be reinvested in educational services and shunt it to investor profits. These profits take concrete form as the limousines, jet airplanes, and mansions that public tax money provides to rich investors. These profits also take symbolic form as they are used to hire public relations firms to influence parents, communities, and other investors to have faith in the company. This is a parasitical financial relationship that results in the management of the schools in ways that will maximize the potential profit for investors while cutting costs. This has tended to result in anti-unionism, the reduction of education to the most measurable and replicable forms, assaults on teacher autonomy, and so on. There is no evidence that the draining of public wealth and its siphoning to capitalists has improved public education or that it is required for the improvement of public education. If the state is going to use privatization as a tool (as the advocates of the Third Way in the United Kingdom do), then it could exercise authoritative state action directly in ways that do not upwardly redistribute wealth or funnel such wealth into misrepresenting the effects of privatization. Moreover, such a redistribution over economic control shifts the collective control over the processes of teaching and learning to the owner or private manager of the privatized educational approach. It captures such educational labor and channels it toward profit making for owners in the short term and future exploitable capitalist labor relations in the long term.

2. **Public versus private cultural politics:** privatization affects the politics of the curriculum. A for-profit company and a nonprofit dependent on a private venture philanthropy cannot have a critical curriculum that makes central, for example, the ways privatization threatens democratic values and ideals. Although most public schools do not have wide-ranging critical curricula, the crucial issue is that some do, and most could. This is a matter of public struggle. Privatization forecloses such struggle by shifting

control to private hands and framing out possibilities that are contrary to institutional and structural interest. The possibility of developing and expanding critical pedagogical practices is a major casualty of privatization. Democratic society requires citizens capable of debate, deliberation, dissent, and the tools of intellectual engagement. Privatization fosters antidemocratic instrumental and transmission-oriented approaches to pedagogy. The privatization of mass media represents an important parallel to the privatization of public schooling with regard to cultural politics. For-profit media disallows representations and questioning that runs counter to the institutional interests.[30] The overemphasis on standards and standardization, testing, and "accountability" replicates a corporate logic in which measurable task performance and submission to authority become central. Intellectual curiosity, investigation, teacher autonomy, and critical pedagogy, not to mention critical theory, have no place in this view. "Critical" in this context means not merely problem-solving skills but the skills and dispositions for criticizing how particular claims to truth secure particular forms of authority. Democratic forms of education enable critical forms of agency, fostering political interpretation that can form the basis for collective social action. Critical curriculum and school models could provide the means for theorizing and acting to challenge the very labor exploitation to which schools such as these prepare students to submit.

3. **Public versus private forms of publicity and privacy including secrecy and transparency:** private companies are able to keep much of what they do secret. EMOs and charters that straddle the line between public and private selectively reveal financial and performance data that would further their capacity to lure investors. Such manipulation is endemic to privatization schemes. Such secrecy represents a tactic on the part of privatizers to disallow collective control over school financing and budgets. The secrecy of privatization prevents collective educational labor for common benefit.

4. **Public versus private forms of selfhood:** privatization produces social relations defined through capitalist reproduction that function pedagogically to instantiate habits of docility and submission to authority at odds with collective control, dialogue, debate, dissent, and other public democratic practices. Privatization fosters individualization in part by encouraging everyone to understand education as a private service primarily about maximizing one's own capacity for competition. This runs counter

to valuing public schooling for the benefit to all. A new common school movement can be involved with producing a new public person imbued with the capacity to recognize and value the collective labor of social life and imagine ways of common benefit from such labor.

In both the neoliberal and liberal visions of schooling, the collective labor of teaching and learning aims for accommodation to the existing economic structure and political forms that foster it. This is an economic structure that individualizes benefit from such labor. The task ahead for the critical perspective is to imagine pedagogical practices, curriculum, and school organization that enact the global commons. How can critical pedagogy make central common labor for common benefit? What path should teachers and students take with communities in recovering control over the work of teaching and learning? How can the struggle against corporate school reform not simply demand limits on testing and a cessation to privatization in all its guises but also demand that public education be the basis for reimagining the economy in truly democratic forms, reimagining the political system and political action not beholden to purchased and commercialized elections, and reimagining the culture as a public rather than a private one.

Corporate school reform threatens the possibility of public schools developing as places where knowledge, pedagogical authority, and experiences are taken up in relation to broader political, ethical, cultural, and material struggles informing competing claims to truth. Although the battle for critical public schools and against privatization and other manifestations of neoliberalism are valuable struggles in themselves, they should also be viewed as an interim goal to what ought to be the broader goals of developing practices, modes of organizing, and habits of social and self-questioning that aim toward the redistribution of state and corporate power from elites to the public while expanding critical consciousness and a radically democratic ethos.

A new common school movement has an inevitably hopeful dimension to it. The common can be built and expanded and can never be fully enclosed because there are parts of human experience that can't be turned into property and have to be held in common. Compassion, ideas, and the planet itself must be held in common.

A first step for educators and others committed to equality and justice to enact a new common school movement is to propagate some key "talking points" to transform public discourse about public education.

Talking Points

- Corporate school reform has failed. Charters, vouchers, privatization, and educational management companies have failed to come through on what they promised—namely, higher "student achievement" and lower costs.
- Corporate school reform worsens racial segregation.[31]
- Corporate school reform deepens inequality in educational resources.
- Corporate school reform introduces a new "audit culture" and "new market bureaucracy" that is expensive, misdirects educational resources, and promotes misery and inefficiency.
- Corporate school reform has no way of dealing with ecological crises.
- Corporate school reform is linked to the values of an economic system designed to expand profit and consumerism over human values such as love, care, and common living.
- As the capitalist economy falters, why should control over education be handed over to business people?
- As the corporate sector realizes the limitations of corporate bureaucracy, why should schooling inherit what doesn't work for business?
- We need a new commitment to public education for public rather than corporate values.

NOTES

Chapter One

1. The visions of the right-wing think tanks such as AEI, Hoover, and Heritage are made particularly clear by Andy Smarick, "The Turnaround Fallacy," *Education Next* 10, 1 (2010). Smarick suggests that public schools should be thought of as private businesses competing against one another and, most important, suggests that the "advantage" of charter schools is that they can be easily closed and replaced with other privatized solutions. Paul T. Hill of the Center on Reinventing Public Education regularly champions this aim in advocating "urban portfolio districts."

2. G. Miron, review of "Charter Schools: A Report on Rethinking the Federal Role in Education," Boulder, CO: National Education Policy Center, retrieved March 13, 2011, from http://nepc.colorado.edu/thinktank/review-charter-federal; A. Molnar, G. Miron, and J. L. Urschel, *Profiles of For-Profit Education Management Organizations: Twelfth Annual Report, 2009–2010,* Boulder, CO: National Education Policy Center, retrieved March 13, 2011, from http://nepc.colorado.edu/publication/EMO-FP-09-10; C. Murray, op-ed: "Why Charter Schools Fail the Test," *New York Times,* retrieved May 4, 2010, from www.nytimes.com/2010/05/05/opinion/05murray.html; V. Byrnes, "Getting a Feel for the Market: The Use of Privatized School Management in Philadelphia," *American Journal of Education* 115 (2009), 437–455; P. E. Peterson and M. M. Chingos, *Impact of For-Profit and Nonprofit Management on Student Achievement: The Philadelphia Intervention 2002–2008,* Working Paper PEPG 09-02, Cambridge, MA: Harvard University, Program on Education Policy and Governance, 2009.

3. See Kevin G. Welner, *Neo-Vouchers: The Emergence of Tuition Tax Credits for Private Schooling,* Lanham, MD: Rowman and Littlefield, 2008.

4. See Patricia Burch, *Hidden Markets: The New Education Privatization,* New York:

Routledge, 2009. For the most thorough tracking of commercialism see Alex Molnar's Schoolhouse Commercialism annual reports available at www.nepc.colorado.edu.

5. Turnaround consulting in schools has been based not on evidence of effectiveness or a cohesive program but rather on a metaphor of corporate turnaround consulting and a massive public subsidy for this market experiment. For excellent coverage of the appalling lack of public oversight see Sam Dillon, "Inexperienced Companies Chase U.S. School Funds," *New York Times,* August 9, 2010, available online at www.nytimes.com; see also my discussion of Alvarez and Marsal's "turnaround consulting" that slashed millions in funding for public schools while netting millions in consulting fees in New Orleans before and after Hurricane Katrina in Kenneth J. Saltman, *Capitalizing on Disaster: Taking and Breaking Public Schools,* Boulder, CO: Paradigm, 2007.

6. Kenneth J. Saltman, "Urban School Decentralization and the Growth of 'Portfolio Districts,'" June 2010, *Great Lakes Center for Education Research and Practice,* available online at www.greatlakescenter.org.

7. I take this up in Kenneth J. Saltman, *The Gift of Education: Public Education and Venture Philanthropy,* New York: Palgrave Macmillan, 2010.

8. Kenneth J. Saltman, "'Value Added' Assessment: Tool for Improvement or Educational 'Nuclear Option,'" September 14, 2010, www.truthout.org; Eva L. Baker, Paul E. Barton, Linda Darling-Hammond, Edward Haertel, Helen F. Ladd, Robert L. Linn, Diane Ravitch, Richard Rothstein, Richard J. Shavelson, and Lorrie A. Shepard, "Problems with the Use of Student Test Scores to Evaluate Teachers," EPI Briefing Paper #278, August 29, 2010, available at www.epi.org.

9. Patricia Burch, *Hidden Markets: The New Education Privatization,* New York: Routledge, 2009.

10. William C. Symonds, "Special Report Education a New Push to Privatize," *Businessweek,* January 14, 2002.

11. Usually such pillage is described as introducing "private sector" efficiencies, which fits the classic definition of ideology as a camera obscura inverting reality as private sector involvement skims wealth out of the system. McKinsey, whose education sector is headed by globe-trotting neoliberal consultant Michael Barber, makes the agenda quite clear: "Drive productivity gains in the public and regulated sectors. Public and regulated sectors such as health care and education represent more than 20 percent of the US economy, but has persistently low productivity growth. McKinsey analysis has demonstrated that, if the US public sector could halve the estimated efficiency gap with similar private sector organizational functions, its productivity would be 5 to 15 percent higher and would generate annual savings of $100 billion to $300 billion." Available at www.mckinsey.com/mgi/publications/growth_and_renewal_in_the_us/index.asp.

12. S. L. Robertson, "Globalisation, GATS, and Trading in Education Services," in *Supranational Regimes and National Education Policies—Encountering Challenge,* ed. J. Kall and R. Rinne. Helsinki: Finnish Education Research Association, 2006; S. Robertson and R. Dale, "The World Bank, the IMF, and the Possibilities of Critical Education," in *International Handbook of Critical Education,* New York: Routledge, 2009.

13. See the work of James Tooley, a scholar at the center of the World Bank educational privatization push, including as James Tooley, *The Beautiful Tree,* Washington, DC: Cato Institute Press, 2009.

14. Greg Toppo, "Union Claims Filipino Teachers Put in 'Virtual Servitude' in Louisiana," *USA Today,* October 1, 2009, available at www.usatoday.com; Kenneth J. Saltman, *Capitalizing on Disaster: Taking and Breaking Public Schools,* Boulder, CO: Paradigm, 2007.

15. Kenneth J. Saltman, *Collateral Damage: Corporatizing Public Schools—A Threat to Democracy,* Lanham, MD: Rowman and Littlefield, 2000; and Henry A. Giroux, *The Terror of Neoliberalism,* Boulder, CO: Paradigm, 2005.

16. The financial bailouts of 2008 for the banks and auto industries did not put U.S. citizens in a significantly greater amount of debt, but the decision by the Bush and Obama administrations to bail out business and not bail out homeowners, students, and those saddled with massive debts from the fraudulent housing bubble did worsen indebtedness for an inordinate number of citizens while redistributing the burden for vast and unprecedented corporate profits onto individuals. In this sense, what was accomplished in part through the bailouts but also through regressive tax policy and corporate welfare was a vast redistribution of wealth upward.

17. See Alex Molnar, Gary Miron, and Jessica Urschel, "Profiles of For-Profit Educational Management Organizations: Eleventh Annual Report," September 2009, Commercialism in Education Research Unit, available at http://epicpolicy.org/files/08-09%20profiles%20report.pdf.

18. See Kenneth J. Saltman, *Capitalizing on Disaster: Taking and Breaking Public Schools,* Boulder, CO: Paradigm, 2007; and Kenneth J. Saltman, *Schooling and the Politics of Disaster,* New York: Routledge, 2007.

19. For the clearest and most up-to-date coverage of the terrain and scope of public school privatization and commercialization, see Alex Molnar's annual reports on school commercialism online at the Educational Policy Studies Laboratory, available at www.schoolcommercialism.org, as well as Alex Molnar, *School Commercialism,* New York: Routledge, 2005. See also Deron Boyles (ed.), *Schools or Markets? Commercialism, Privatization and School-Business Partnerships,* New York: Lawrence Erlbaum, 2004; Joel Spring, *Educating the Consumer-Citizen,* New York: Lawrence Erlbaum, 2003; and Alfie Kohn and Patrick Shannon (eds.), *Education, Inc.,* Portsmouth, NH: Heinemann, 2002. See also Kenneth Saltman, "Essay Review of *Education, Inc.,*" *Teachers College Record,* 2003.

20. The majority of studies of charter school effects on academic achievement show on par to negative effects in comparison with traditional public schools. Two of the most extensive and significant studies were the 2004 NAEP results, as analyzed by Martin Carnoy, R. Jacobsen, L. Mishel, and R. Rothstein, *The Charter School Dust Up: Examining the Evidence on Enrollment and Achievement,* Washington, DC: Economic Policy Institute, 2005; and the Stanford CREDO study *Multiple Choice: Charter School Performance in 16 States,* 2009, available at http://credo.stanford.edu/reports/MULTIPLE_CHOICE_CREDO.pdf. Other studies include E. Bodine, B. Fuller,

M. González, L. Huerta, S. Naughton, S. Park, and L. W. Teh, "Disparities in Charter School Resources—The Influence of State Policy and Community," *Journal of Education Policy*, 23, 1 (2008): 1–33; K. Finnigan, N. Adelman, L. Anderson, L. Cotton, M. B. Donnelly, and T. Price, *Evaluation of the Public Charter Schools Program: Final Evaluation Report,* Washington, DC: U.S. Department of Education, 2004; H. F. Ladd and R. P. Bifulco, *The Impacts of Charter Schools on Student Achievement: Evidence from North Carolina*, Working Paper SAN04-01, Durham, NC: Terry Sanford Institute of Public Policy, Duke University, 2004; F. H. Nelson, B. Rosenberg, and N. Van Meter, *Charter School Achievement on the 2003 National Assessment of Educational Progress*, Washington, DC: American Federation of Teachers, 2004; What Works Clearinghouse, *WWC Quick Review of the Report "Multiple Choice: Charter School Performance in 16 States,"* Washington, DC: Center for Research on Education Outcomes, 2010.

21. See Kenneth J. Saltman, *The Gift of Education: Public Education and Venture Philanthropy,* New York: Palgrave Macmillan, 2010.

22. See Linda Darling-Hammond, *The Flat World and Education,* New York: Teachers College Press, 2010.

23. My lecture was delivered October 27, 2009, at the Richland Arts Center in Rayville, Louisiana, and was sponsored by the Louisiana School Board Association, which provided my flight. The event was covered by the *News-Star* in the article "Educators Discuss Private Influence," November 15, 2009. The head of the Louisiana Association of Public Charter Schools, Caroline Roemer Shirley, attacked me in an op-ed in the *News-Star* in which she falsely claimed that nonprofit charters are not a kind of privatization and that EdisonLearning and SABIS exemplify for-profit excellence. The *News-Star* would not respond to my request to respond to Roemer Shirley's op-ed on my own, so I posted my response in multiple segments on an open source commentary attached to the op-ed. The op-ed and my response appear to have been removed from the newspaper's website.

24. Andy Smarick, "The Turnaround Fallacy," *Education Next* 10, 1 (2010).

25. Kenneth Saltman, *Capitalizing on Disaster: Taking and Breaking Public Schools,* Boulder, CO: Paradigm, 2007, p. 32.

26. Richard Lee Colvin, "Chapter 1: A New Generation of Philanthropists and Their Great Ambitions," in *With the Best of Intentions*, ed. Frederick Hess, Cambridge, MA: Harvard Education Press, 2005, p. 21.

27. Rick Cohen, "Strategic Grantmaking: Foundations and the School Privatization Movement," *National Committee for Responsive Philanthropy,* November 2007, p. 5, available at www.ncrp.org/index.php?option-com_ixxocart&Itemid-41&p-product&id-4&parent-3.

28. See, for example, Kenneth Saltman, *Collateral Damage: Corporatizing Public Schools—A Threat to Democracy*, Lanham, MD: Rowman and Littlefield, 2000; *The Edison Schools: Corporate Schooling and the Assault on Public Education*, New York: Routledge, 2005; and *Capitalizing on Disaster: Taking and Breaking Public Schools*, Boulder, CO: Paradigm, 2007.

29. As an economic doctrine, neoliberalism calls for the privatization of public goods and services, the deregulation of markets, foreign direct investment, and monetarism. Neoliberalism represents an ideology of market fundamentalism in which the inevitably bureaucratically encumbered state can do no good, and markets must be relied upon to

do what the state has formerly done. Neoliberalism imagines the social world as privatized and suggests that economic rationality ought to be expanded to every last realm. In this view, the public sector disappears as the only legitimate collectivities can be markets while the individual is principally defined as an economic actor, that is, a worker or consumer. The state in this view ought to use its power to facilitate markets. Democracy becomes an administrative matter best left to markets rather than to public deliberation.

30. Pierre Bourdieu, *Firing Back: Against the Tyranny of the Market,* New York: New Press, 2003.

31. See Joel Spring, *Educating the Consumer-Citizen,* New York: Lawrence Erlbaum, 2003.

32. The Chicago Reader has an archive of Joravsky's articles on TIFs at www.chicagoreader.org.

33. See Dorothy Shipps, *School Reform Corporate Style: Chicago 1880–2000,* Lawrence: University Press of Kansas, 2006.

34. Available online at www.latimes.com/news/local/teachers-investigation/.

35. A search on Academic Search Premiere retrieved September 9, 2010, found only 33 scholarly peer-reviewed articles on a search of "value-added assessment," with several of these being unrelated to the search topic, and only 7 empirically based studies. A search of "value-added model" found 60 scholarly peer reviewed articles, but these overlap with the "value-added assessment" articles. To put in perspective how small a body of scholarly research this is, a search on "charter schools" nets 578 scholarly peer reviewed articles. The paucity of research ought to be a warning considering the massive impact of the adoption of the reform.

36. See Eva L. Baker et al., "Problems with the Use of Student Test Scores to Evaluate Teachers," EPI Briefing Paper #276, August 29, 2010, available at http://epi.3cdn.net/724cd9a1eb91c40ff0_hwm6iij90.pdf.

37. I detail the efforts of the Bill and Melinda Gates Foundation and the Eli and Edythe Broad Foundation to push for the implementation of teacher evaluations linked to student test scores in my book *The Gift of Education: Public Education and Venture Philanthropy,* New York: Palgrave Macmillan, 2010.

38. For recent criticisms of VAM see Eva L. Baker et al., "Problems with the Use of Student Test Scores to Evaluate Teachers," EPI Briefing Paper #276, August 29, 2010, available at http://epi.3cdn.net/724cd9a1eb91c40ff0_hwm6iij90.pdf; Gerald Bracey, "Value-Added Models Front and Center," *Phi Delta Kappan* 87, 6 (February 2006), pp. 478–479; and Jennifer L. Jennings and Sean P. Corcoran, "Beware of Geeks Bearing Formulas," *Phi Delta Kappan* 90, 9 (May 2009), pp. 635–639.

39. Carl Bialik, "Needs Improvement: Where Teacher Report Cards Fall Short," *Wall Street Journal,* August 21, 2010, available at http://online.wsj.com/article/SB10001424052748704476104575440100517520516.html?KEYWORDS-needs+improvement.

40. On the cultural politics of the soap industry, see Anne McLintock, *Imperial Leather: Race, Gender, and Sexuality in the Colonial Contest,* New York: Routledge, 1995.

41. Rick Dasog, "BP Aids State's School Content," *Sacramento Bee,* September 7, 2010, p. 1A, available online at www.sacbee.com/2010/09/07/3009448/bp-aids

-statesschool-content.html#storylink-scinlineshare. As Robin Truth Goodman and I have detailed, this is not BP's first foray into teaching children about science, nature, and the environment. See Kenneth J. Saltman and Robin Truth Goodman, "Rivers of Fire: BPAmoco's Impact on Education," in Kenneth J. Saltman and David Gabbard, *Education as Enforcement: The Militarization and Corporatization of Schools,* 2nd ed., New York: Routledge, 2010.

42. For recent international comparative case studies and compiled research see Linda Darling-Hammond, *The Flat World and Education,* New York: Teachers College Press, 2010. While valuable informationally in this regard Darling-Hammond wraps her arguments for equalizing funding and desegregation in a global vision defined by neoliberalism—hence the title taken from neoliberal journalist Thomas L. Friedman of the *New York Times.* I take this up at length in Chapter 4.

43. See Henry Giroux, *Youth in a Suspect Society: Democracy or Disposability?* New York: Palgrave Macmillan, 2009.

44. For my recent extended criticism of both the neoliberal and vulgar Marxist reduction of education to economism see Kenneth J. Saltman, *The Gift of Education: Public Education and Venture Philanthropy,* New York: Palgrave Macmillan, 2010, Chapter 6, "Education Beyond Economism."

45. See Henry Giroux, *Teachers as Intellectuals,* Westport, CT: Bergin and Garvey, 1988.

46. For extensive empirical evidence on teacher pay, teacher turnover, and state and international comparisons see Linda Darling-Hammond, *The Flat World and Education,* New York: Teachers College Press, 2010. Despite the valuable information, Darling-Hammond unfortunately wraps her liberal national arguments for equalizing educational resources in a neoliberal international perspective that presumes a national goal of necessary global economic competition.

47. See Deborah Curtis, Deborah Bordelon, and Kenneth Teitelbaum, "Keep a Focus on Meaningful Reform Agendas Instead of Political Agendas," *Planning and Change* 41, 3/4 (2010), pp. 133–146.

48. Ibid.

49. I take this up in the context of public school privatization in Kenneth J. Saltman, *The Edison Schools: Corporate Schooling and the Assault on Public Education,* New York: Routledge, 2005. In the context of corporate media see John Nichols and Robert McChesney, *The Death and Life of American Journalism,* New York: Nation Books, 2011. The ideological limits imposed through political economy is taken up by Edward Herman and Noam Chomsky, *Manufacturing Consent,* and much of the critical media work of Sut Jhally. The important mass communications scholarship that has addressed the relationship between ownership and content (Herbert Shiller, Dallas Smythe, and so on) has been pushed out of communications curriculum in higher education as the field has become intensely commercially oriented and heavily reliant upon corporate "partnerships" as courses in public relations and telecommunications expand. This fact further supports the point. See also Henry Giroux and Grace Pollock, *The Mouse that Roared: Disney and the End of Innocence,* 2nd ed., Lanham, MD: Rowman and Littlefield, 2010.

50. See Henry Giroux's crucial distinction between teachers as traditional, critical, and transformative intellectuals in *Teachers as Intellectuals*, Westport, CT: Bergin and Garvey, 1988.

51. Upon beginning his first term as mayor of Chicago, former Obama chief of staff Rahm Emanuel pledged to double the number of "urban academies" in the third largest district in the United States. These "clinically-oriented," that is practicalist, alternative certification programs receive private foundation grants and government funding that pay teaching trainees $20,000–30,000 while they begin teaching.

52. For critical exposés on the centrality of the venture philanthropists to contemporary U.S. educational policy see Kenneth J. Saltman, *The Gift of Education: Public Education and Venture Philanthropy*, New York: Palgrave Macmillan, 2010; and Philip Kovacs (ed.), *The Gates Foundation and the Future of U.S. "Public" Schooling*, New York: Routledge, 2010.

53. See Kenneth J. Saltman, "The Right-Wing Attack on Critical and Public Education in the United States: From Neoliberalism to Neoconservatism," *Cultural Politics* 2, 3 (November 2006).

54. See Editorial, "Pass/fail/fail/fail," *Chicago Tribune*, June 26, 2011, p. 22.

55. See Giroux's *Stormy Weather*, Boulder, CO: Paradigm, 2006; Zygmunt Bauman's *Wasted Lives*, Boston: Polity, 2004; and also Jean Baudrillard's *Consumer Society*, Thousand Oaks, CA: Sage, 1998.

56. See "Afterword" in the paperback edition of Slavoj Zizek, *Living in the End Times*, New York: Verso, 2011.

57. Giroux takes this up brilliantly in the video "Culture, Politics, and Pedagogy," Media Education Foundation, 2006, preview available online at www.mediaed.org/cgi-bin/commerce.cgi?preadd-action&key-130.

58. See, for example, Joel Spring, *Educating the Consumer-Citizen*, Mahwah, NJ: Lawrence Erlbaum Assoc. Inc., 2003; and Dorothy Shipps, *School Reform Corporate Style*, Lawrence: University Press of Kansas, 2006.

59. Thomas L. Friedman, "The New Untouchables," *New York Times*, October 20, 2009, p. A31.

60. See Henry Giroux, "Introduction: Expendable Futures: Youth and Democracy at Risk" and "In the Shadow of the Gilded Age," in *Youth in a Suspect Society: Democracy or Disposability?* New York: Palgrave Macmillan, 2009.

61. "The Cost of a Soldier Deployed in Afghanistan," Marketplace Morning Report, February 22, 2011, available at http://marketplace.publicradio.org/display/web/2011/02/22/am-the-cost-of-a-soldier-deployed-in-afghanistan/.

Chapter Two

1. Neither the advocates of portfolio districts such as Paul T. Hill nor liberals such as Henry Levin interested in efficacy nor I with my critical focus on questions of politics and ethics find that there is much hope of developing a method to assess the success or failure of urban portfolio districts. See P. Hill, C. Campbell, and D. Menefee-Libey,

Portfolio School Districts for Big Cities: An Interim Report, Seattle: Center on Reinventing Public Education, University of Washington, 2009. See also the liberal collection by Katrina Bulkley, Jeffrey Henig, and Henry Levin (eds.), *Between Public and Private: Politics, Governance, and the New Portfolio Models for Urban School Reform,* Cambridge, MA: Harvard Education Press, 2010.

2. P. Hill, C. Campbell, and D. Menefee-Libey, *Portfolio School Districts for Big Cities: An Interim Report.* Seattle: Center on Reinventing Public Education, University of Washington, 2009, p. 6.

3. It is important to note here that empirical studies of the elements of portfolio district reform begin with theoretical assumptions and values. In pointing out the lack of empirically based study of the portfolio model and its elements, I do not intend to suggest that empirical studies are inherently superior to other kinds of policy scholarship or to suggest that "numbers speak for themselves." Empirical studies begin with particular framing assumptions that require adequate theorization. Good, empirically based scholarship in the social sciences sufficiently theorizes the researcher's assumptions. The historical tendency toward radical objectivism, which brackets out the researcher's subjective position and its influence on the framing assumptions of the study, is referred to as *positivism.* Positivism has been thoroughly criticized in education. See, for example, H. A. Giroux, *Theory and Resistance in Education,* Westport, CT: Bergin and Garvey, 1983.

4. Non-peer-reviewed reports that advocate for portfolio districts but do not contain empirical evidence and are not based on scholarly study include P. Hill, C. Campbell, and D. Menefee-Libey, *Portfolio School Districts for Big Cities: An Interim Report,* Seattle: Center on Reinventing Public Education, University of Washington, 2009; A. Cavanna, J. Olchefske, and S. Fleischman, "The Potential of the Portfolio Approach," *Educational Leadership* 63, 8 (2006), pp. 89–91; and J. M. Brodie, "Study: Portfolio Districts 'Promising Works in Progress,'" *Education Daily* 42, 173 (October 8, 2009), pp. 1–3. There are no peer-reviewed empirical studies that do or do not advocate for portfolio districts.

5. As the CRPE website (www.crpe.org/cs/crpe/print/csr_docs/home.htm) states, the public schools often "fail to achieve this goal" of educating all students well. The goal of improving public education is not found in strengthening the public aspects but making the public system look more like a private system through a number of means, including competition, choice, and corporate-style management.

6. P. Wohlstetter and K. McCurdy, "The Link Between School Decentralization and School Politics," *Urban Education* 25, 4 (January 1991), pp. 391–414.

7. Ibid.

8. S. Grosskopf and C. Moutray, "Evaluating Performance in Chicago Public High Schools in the Wake of Decentralization," *Economics of Education Review* 20 (2001), pp. 1–14.

9. A crucial difference between the "old" and "new" decentralization involves the shift away from teacher autonomy particularly under chartering. On the emphasis of teacher autonomy under the "old" decentralization, see, for example, P. A. White,

"Teacher Empowerment Under 'Ideal' School Site Autonomy," *Educational Evaluation and Policy Analysis* 14, 1 (Spring 1992), pp. 69–82. The deunionizing effects of chartering in particular as well as the rise of outcomes-based and test-based forms of accountability result in a shift away from teacher autonomy that makes the "new" decentralization nearly diametrically opposed to the "old" in terms of teacher control.

10. See J. R. Henig and W. C. Rich (eds.), *Mayors in the Middle: Politics, Race, and Mayoral Control of Urban Schools*, Princeton, NJ: Princeton University Press, 2003. See also S. Grosskopf and C. Moutray, "Evaluating Performance in Chicago Public High Schools in the Wake of Decentralization," *Economics of Education Review* 20 (2001), pp. 1–14.

11. William G. Ouchi, "Power to the Principals: Decentralization in Three Large School Districts," *Organization Science* 17, 2 (2006), pp. 298–307, contends that the crucial determination for the success of decentralization is principal control over spending. His study claims to show student achievement improvements in principal-strong decentralization merged with school autonomy over "staffing, scheduling, and teaching methods" and leaving "instructional decisions to the schools and then audit them carefully." His study involves Edmonton, Alberta, Houston, and Seattle. The portfolio district model emphasizes mayoral or state takeover capitalizing on crisis or disaster to initiate the model and then "the portfolio idea is put into action by unconventional leadership teams led by lawyers, MBAs, public policy experts, or educators with unconventional backgrounds, for example Teach for America alumni. These actors are often recruited from lucrative careers elsewhere; they don't appear on the lists assembled by headhunters who serve traditional local school boards." In P. Hill, C. Campbell, and D. Menefee-Libey, *Portfolio School Districts for Big Cities: An Interim Report*, Seattle: Center on Reinventing Public Education, University of Washington, 2009, p. 8. The strong principal control emphasized by Ouchi and to which he attributes his good results is not explicitly a part of the mayoral/state/leadership team control emphasized by the Center on Reinventing Public Education.

12. P. Hill, C. Campbell, and D. Menefee-Libey, *Portfolio School Districts for Big Cities: An Interim Report*, Seattle: Center on Reinventing Public Education, University of Washington, 2009.

13. Ibid., p. 6.

14. The idea of taking advantage of disaster for radical market-based educational experimentation predated Hurricane Katrina in 2005, but that disaster was seized upon in mass media and policy circles to call for a radical market-based experiment in educational rebuilding. Paul Hill, who is the leading author advocating portfolio districts and its strategy of creative destruction, also authored an influential report with Jane Hannaway that called for refusing to rebuild the New Orleans public schools and instead putting in place privatized educational schemes. See P. Hill and J. Hannaway, *The Future of Public Education in New Orleans*, Washington, DC: Urban Institute, 2006, retrieved May 26, 2010, from www.urban.org/UploadedPDF/900913_public_education.pdf/. I critically detail this post-Katrina history in K. J. Saltman, *Capitalizing on Disaster: Taking and Breaking Public Schools*, Boulder, CO: Paradigm, 2007, Chapter 1, "Silver Linings and

Golden Opportunities." This is also taken up by Naomi Klein, *The Shock Doctrine*, New York: Metropolitan Books, 2007.

15. Academic Search Premiere searches were conducted on terms included in Tables 2.1, 2.2, and 2.3. My search for "portfolio school district" returned three articles. None of these offers evidence on academic achievement or cost. "Portfolio district" returned three relevant articles, none of which has evidence. "Portfolio school" returned three relevant articles that overlap with the other searches but that do not contain evidence. None of these searches yield any scholarly peer-reviewed studies. An Academic Search Premiere search of "charter schools" and "cost" found eight peer-reviewed journal articles between 2002–2009, but none of these contained study of cost comparisons between charters and traditional public schools. An Academic Search Premiere search of "No Child Left Behind" and "student achievement" found fifty-three scholarly peer-reviewed articles with full text available. Although several articles pointed to the failure of NCLB to achieve what it was designed to achieve, namely raising student achievement or decreasing the so-called achievement gap between white students and racial minority students, the majority of studies pointed to a number of methodological, theoretical, and practical problems with high-stakes test-based forms of accountability. None of these studies could be understood as framing NCLB as successful in terms of its aims. Searches for Table 2.1 included cross-referencing city and district names with variations on "portfolio district" and also cross-searching "student achievement" and also "cost" with these variations. Search terms for Table 2.2 are listed in the table.

16. The majority of studies of charter school effects on academic achievement show on par to negative effects in comparison with traditional public schools. Two of the most extensive and significant studies were the 2004 NAEP results as analyzed by Martin Carnoy, R. Jacobsen, L. Mishel, and R. Rothstein, *The Charter School Dust Up: Examining the Evidence on Enrollment and Achievement*, Washington, DC: Economic Policy Institute, 2005; and the Stanford CREDO study *Disparities in Charter School Resources—The Influence of State Policy and Community*, 2009, available at http://credo .stanford.edu/reports/MULTIPLE_CHOICE_CREDO.pdf. See also Chapter 1, endnote 20, for other notable studies.

17. P. Hill, C. Campbell, and D. Menefee-Libey, *Portfolio School Districts for Big Cities: An Interim Report*, Seattle: Center on Reinventing Public Education, University of Washington, 2009, p. 46. The authors of the report write, "It is unlikely, however, that we can ever give a simple answer to the question, 'Have the cities that adopted a portfolio strategy benefited from it?' This is so for several reasons, including that districts started in different places and moved at different paces toward full implementation. For example, in 2005 and 2006, New Orleans had no alternative to opening schools in partnership with independent providers. If only in the sense that the portfolio approach let the state provide schools where none existed, the approach must be counted as a success. In the other cities, where children could find schools to attend before the district adopted the portfolio approach, no such judgment is possible." Although I agree with the difficulties of measuring the portfolio district approach, it is difficult to see how the authors nonetheless both argue for test-based accountability and call for implementing the

model without this evidence. Moreover, the claim in this quote that New Orleans "had no alternative to opening schools in partnership with independent providers" somehow neglects to mention that immediately after Katrina, Paul Hill played an active role in advocating to administrators and legislators that the New Orleans schools not be rebuilt and that instead the system be privatized. See P. Hill and J. Hannaway, *The Future of Public Education in New Orleans,* Washington, DC: Urban Institute, 2006, retrieved May 26, 2010, from www.urban.org/UploadedPDF/900913_public_education.pdf. For an elaborate analysis of how the market-oriented think tanks used the natural disaster in the Gulf Coast to further a long-standing privatization agenda for charters, vouchers, and no-bid contracting, see K. J. Saltman, *Capitalizing on Disaster: Taking and Breaking Public Schools,* Boulder, CO: Paradigm, 2007, Chapter 1, "Silver Linings and Golden Opportunities." For additional evidence regarding post-Katrina New Orleans, see K. E. Bulkley, *Review of "Fix the City Schools: Moving All Schools to Charter-like Autonomy,"* Boulder, CO, and Tempe, AZ: Education and the Public Interest Center and Education Policy Research Unit, 2010, retrieved May 26, 2010, from http://epicpolicy.org/ thinktank/review-fix-city-schools.

18. For one of the few examples of a project specifically aiming for such critical engagement see Kristen Buras, *Pedagogy, Politics, and the Privatized City: Stories of Dispossession and Defiance from New Orleans,* New York: Teachers College Press, 2010.

19. See, for example, K. E. Bulkley, *Review of "Fix the City Schools: Moving All Schools to Charter-like Autonomy,"* Boulder, CO, and Tempe, AZ: Education and the Public Interest Center and Education Policy Research Unit, 2010, retrieved May 26, 2010, from http://epicpolicy.org/thinktank/review-fix-city-schools; and G. Miron and B. Applegate, *Review of "Multiple Choice: Charter School Performance in 16 States,"* Boulder, CO, and Tempe, AZ: Education and the Public Interest Center and Education Policy Research Unit, 2009, retrieved April 2, 2010, from http://epicpolicy.org/thinktank/ review-multiple-choice. On Louisiana see also Senator Thomas Robichaux, "Louisiana Schools Improved, But Who Is Responsible?" *Bayou Buzz,* October 19, 2009, available at www.bayoubuzz.com/News/Louisiana/Government/Louisiana_Schools_Improved_ But_Who_Is_Responsible_9670.asp. See also E. Sullivan and D. Morgan, *Pushed Out: Harsh Discipline in Louisiana Schools Denies the Right to Education,* New York and New Orleans: National Economic and Social Rights Initiative, and Families and Friends of Louisiana's Incarcerated Children, 2010. The latter raises important issues regarding RSD public and charter school pushouts and the implications for claims about performance. See also the important work on New Orleans and Louisiana by Kristen Buras.

20. An Academic Search Premiere search for "portfolio school district" returned three articles, none of which offer evidence on academic achievement or cost. "Portfolio district" returned three relevant articles, none of which have evidence. "Portfolio school" returned three relevant articles that overlap with the other searches but that do not contain evidence. None of these searches yielded any scholarly peer-reviewed studies. Non-peer-reviewed reports that advocate for portfolio districts but do not contain evidence include P. Hill, C. Campbell, and D. Menefee-Libey, *Portfolio School Districts for Big Cities: An Interim Report,* Seattle: Center on Reinventing Public Education,

University of Washington, 2009; A. Cavanna, J. Olchefske, and S. Fleischman, "The Potential of the Portfolio Approach," *Educational Leadership* 63, 8 (2006), pp. 89–91; and J. M. Brodie, "Study: Portfolio Districts 'Promising Works in Progress,'" *Education Daily* 42, 173 (2009), pp. 1–3.

21. P. Hill, C. Campbell, and D. Menefee-Libey, *Portfolio School Districts for Big Cities: An Interim Report,* Seattle: Center on Reinventing Public Education, University of Washington, 2009, p. 10.

22. Ibid., p. 9.

23. Ibid., p. 46.

24. Ibid.

25. Ibid., p. 47.

26. Ibid.

27. Ibid.

28. Ibid., pp. 47–48.

29. S. Banchero, "Daley School Plan Fails to Make Grade," *Chicago Tribune,* January 17, 2010, p. 1.

30. Ibid.

31. D. Humphrey, V. Young, K. Bosetti, L. Cassidy, E. Rivera, H. Wang, S. Murray, and M. Wechsler, *Renaissance Schools Fund-Supported Schools: Early Outcomes, Challenges, and Opportunities,* Menlo Park, CA: SRI International, 2009, retrieved May 26, 2010, from http://policyweb.sri.com/cep/publications/RSF_FINAL_April_15v2.pdf.

32. S. Banchero, "Daley School Plan Fails to Make Grade," *Chicago Tribune,* January 17, 2010, p. 1.

33. Ibid.

34. Ibid.

35. The Stanford CREDO study *Disparities in Charter School Resources—The Influence of State Policy and Community* is available at http://credo.stanford.edu/reports/MULTIPLE_CHOICE_CREDO.pdf.

36. See, for example, G. Miron and B. Applegate, *Review of "Multiple Choice: Charter School Performance in 16 States,"* Boulder, CO, and Tempe, AZ: Education and the Public Interest Center and Education Policy Research Unit, 2009, retrieved April 2, 2010, from http://epicpolicy.org/thinktank/review-multiple-choice. On Louisiana see also Senator Thomas Robichaux, "Louisiana Schools Improved, But Who Is Responsible?" *Bayou Buzz,* October 19, 2009, available at www.bayoubuzz.com/News/Louisiana/Government/Louisiana_Schools_Improved_But_Who_Is_Responsible_9670.asp.

37. P. Hill, C. Campbell, and D. Menefee-Libey, *Portfolio School Districts for Big Cities: An Interim Report,* Seattle: Center on Reinventing Public Education, University of Washington, 2009, p. 39.

38. Ibid.

39. Ibid., p. 40.

40. See K. J. Saltman, *The Gift of Education: Public Education and Venture Philanthropy,* New York: Palgrave Macmillan, 2010.

41. An Academic Search Premiere search of "charter schools" and "cost" found eight peer-reviewed journal articles between 2002–2009, but none of these contained study of cost comparisons between charters and traditional public schools.

42. An Academic Search Premiere search of "No Child Left Behind" and "student achievement" found fifty-three scholarly peer-reviewed articles with full text available. While several articles pointed to the failure of NCLB to achieve what it was designed to achieve, namely raising student achievement or decreasing the so-called achievement gap between white students and racial minority students, the majority of studies pointed to a number of methodological, theoretical, and practical problems with high-stakes test-based forms of accountability. None of these studies could be understood as framing NCLB as successful in terms of its aims. For an overview of the failure of NCLB with regard to fulfilling its student achievement aspirations and a helpful review of literature on this, see H. Shirvani, "Does the No Child Left Behind Act Leave Some Children Behind?" *International Journal of Learning* 16, 3 (2009), pp. 49–57.

43. The idea of a racial/ethnic "achievement gap" is problematic in much the same way as that of "student achievement." An achievement gap presupposes that knowledge deemed universally valuable is being insufficiently distributed equitably. This framing of knowledge has no place for local knowledge and student experience as the basis for comprehending how students' lived experiences in and outside of school are generated in part through broader social, political, economic, and cultural forces and formations. Such insights bear on a number of important matters, such as the broader purposes of public schooling and student motivation and agency. Although a number of traditions, such as Deweyan reconstruction, critical pedagogy, and culturally relevant pedagogy, take this up, the current trend toward numerical test-based outputs presumes that the goal is the "enforcement" of the right knowledge ordained by those who know best. This is a view of knowledge that is dogmatic and at odds with how knowledge is conceived at the highest levels of academic learning, in which dialogue, rational exchange, and peer review are central.

44. H. Shirvani, "Does the No Child Left Behind Act Leave Some Children Behind?" *International Journal of Learning* 16, 3 (2009), pp. 49–57.

45. P. Hill, C. Campbell, and D. Menefee-Libey, *Portfolio School Districts for Big Cities: An Interim Report,* Seattle: Center on Reinventing Public Education, University of Washington, 2009, p. 48.

46. See K. J. Saltman, *The Gift of Education: Public Education and Venture Philanthropy,* New York: Palgrave Macmillan, 2010, p. 1.

47. Ibid.

48. For a number of projects initiated in the four major portfolio districts, see P. Hill, C. Campbell, and D. Menefee-Libey, *Portfolio School Districts for Big Cities: An Interim Report,* Seattle: Center on Reinventing Public Education, University of Washington, 2009, p. 31. For the discussion of philanthropic support see pp. 39–40.

49. Available at www.pdaillinois.org/site/node/398.

50. See, for example, J. Blair, D. J. Hoff, B. Keller, and K. K. Manzo, "Teacher Distribution Hurts Poor Schools, AASA Warns," *Education Week* 21, 25 (2002), p. 18,

retrieved April 17, 2010, from Research Library Core, Document ID 110600608. See also Linda Darling-Hammond, *The Flat World and Education*, New York: Teachers College Press, 2010.

51. I take up the privatization efforts of the venture philanthropists in education and the Obama education policy in *The Gift of Education: Public Education and Venture Philanthropy*, New York: Palgrave Macmillan, 2010. That book discusses Secretary of Education Duncan's market-based call for seeing groups of schools as a portfolio. Speaking at the Renaissance Schools Fund "Free to Choose, Free to Succeed: The New Market in Public Education" event, then-CEO of Chicago Public Schools Duncan opened the event by prematurely and unjustifiably celebrating the portfolio district approach in Chicago's Renaissance 2010 and generally. The Center on Reinventing Public Education Interim Report, championing the implementation of portfolio districts on the basis of low public school achievement scores, concludes by stating that, while it will not be possible to definitively measure student achievement gains following implementation, the expansion of "choice" is a way to measure success; see P. Hill, C. Campbell, and D. Menefee-Libey, *Portfolio School Districts for Big Cities: An Interim Report*, Seattle: Center on Reinventing Public Education, University of Washington, 2009, pp. 47–48. Thus, test scores according to CRPE should be used to justify implementing market-based choice schemes, but not to measure the effects of such implementations. Perhaps this is a growing trend of policy experts changing the rules when losing the game, as Charles Murray of the American Enterprise Institute recently put forward a similar assertion that now that privatized voucher schemes are in place and are not faring well in test-based achievement, we should change the criterion by which they are judged. See C. Murray, Op-Ed: "Why Charter Schools Fail the Test," *New York Times*, May 4, 2010, www.nytimes.com/2010/05/05/opinion/05murray.html.

52. V. Byrnes, "Getting a Feel for the Market: The Use of Privatized School Management in Philadelphia," *American Journal of Education* 115 (2009), pp. 437–455; P. E. Peterson and M. M. Chingos, *Impact of For-Profit and Nonprofit Management on Student Achievement: The Philadelphia Intervention 2002–2008*, Working Paper PEPG 09-02, Cambridge, MA: Harvard University, Program on Education Policy and Governance, 2009.

53. See, for example, G. Bracey, *Charter Schools' Performance and Accountability: A Disconnect*, Tempe, AZ: Education Policy Studies Laboratory, 2005, retrieved April 17, 2010, from www.epicpolicy.org/files/EPSL-0505-113-EPRU-exec.pdf.

54. See the Program for International Student Assessment, available at http://nces.ed.g.ov/surveys/pisa.

55. D. C. Berliner and B. J. Biddle, "The Awful Alliance of the Media and Public-School Critics," *Education Digest* 64, 5 (1999), pp. 4–10, retrieved April 17, 2010, from Research Library Core, Document ID: 38003652.

56. See, for example, D. C. Berliner, *Poverty and Potential: Out-of-School Factors and School Success*, Boulder, CO, and Tempe, AZ: Education and the Public Interest Center and Education Policy Research Unit, 2009, retrieved April 17, 2010, from http://epicpolicy.org/publication/poverty-and-potential; or see Jonathan Kozol's extensive works.

57. D. Shipps, *School Reform, Corporate Style: Chicago 1880–2000*. Lawrence: University Press of Kansas, 2006.

58. See, for example, the studies in Linda Darling-Hammond, *The Flat World and Education*, New York: Teachers College Press, 2010.

Chapter Three

1. Kenneth J. Saltman, *Collateral Damage: Corporatizing Public Schools—A Threat to Democracy*, Lanham, MD: Rowman and Littlefield, 2000.

2. See John Nichols and Robert McChesney, *The Life and Death of American Journalism*, New York: Nation Books, 2011.

3. On the radical expansion of news content being composed of public relations see Nichols and McChesney, *The Life and Death of American Journalism*, New York: Nation Books, 2011. This book challenges the suggestion that the decline of journalism has to do with the loss of classified revenues due to the Internet. Instead it makes the compelling case that good journalism has been decimated by corporate media consolidation. The authors contend that the vast majority of online news content is repeated from traditional newspaper reporting. This fact is confirmed by the Pew Research Center's Project for Excellence in Journalism study "How News Happens," January 11, 2010, available at www.journalism.org/analysis report/how news happens. Together these facts suggest that the profit motive applied to news is having an utterly devastating effect on the ability of citizens to get information necessary for self-governance. The implications are enormous for public education at a time in which corporate school reform injects the profit motive into public education.

4. See the work of Alex Molnar, Deron Boyles, and Trevor Norris for excellent studies of contemporary school commercialism.

5. See Henry A. Giroux, "Schooling and the Culture of Positivism: Notes on the Death of History" and "Culture and Rationality in Frankfurt School Thought: Ideological Foundations for a Theory of Social Education," reprinted in *Pedagogy and the Politics of Hope: Theory, Culture, and Schooling*, New York: Westview, 1994.

6. My discussion of the new market positivism and new market bureaucracy is informed by a series of conversations that I had with Alex Means. See Alex Means, *Schooling in the Age of Austerity*, New York: Palgrave Macmillan, 2013.

7. Theodor Adorno, *Introduction to Sociology*, Stanford, CA: Polity Press, 2000.

8. Mark Fisher, *Capitalist Realism: Is There No Alternative?* London: Zero Books, 2008.

9. References to NEPC briefs.

10. John Chubb and Terry Moe, *Politics, Markets, and America's Schools*, Washington, DC: Brookings Institution, 1990.

11. See, for example, Michael Apple, *Ideology and Curriculum*, New York: Routledge, 2006; Henry Giroux, *Theory and Resistance in Education*, Westport, CT: Bergin and Garvey, 1983; and the work of Paul Willis, Stanley Aronowitz, Jean Anyon, Michael

Young, and Geoff Whitty, among others. This scholarship was very much engaged with the work of Pierre Bourdieu's and Louis Althusser's reproduction theories.

12. See Antonio Gramsci, *Selections from the Prison Notebooks,* edited by Quintin Hoare, New York: International Publishers, 1971. A crucial aspect of Gramsci's thought was the insight that for a political bloc to win hegemonic control requires not only the use of coercion through armed insurrection or strike but through the formation of subaltern intellectuals who can rearticulate the particular interests of working-class people into a new common sense. Winning politically means winning educationally for Gramsci. Two particularly valuable uses of Gramsci in the U.S. context in this era are Michael Apple's *Ideology and Curriculum* and Henry Giroux's *Teachers as Intellectuals.*

13. See Raymond Williams, *The Long Revolution,* London: Chatto and Windus, 1961, p. 68. Williams explains how the selection of knowledge and cultural artifacts furthers to educate people into the values and the interests of dominant groups. Such cultural struggle explains why competing views of what constitutes a cannon matter for the fixing of cultural power by particular classes and cultural groups. A particular glaring use of this can be found in the bookstore that shelves Toni Morrison under fiction rather than literature or the tendency of the Common Core Knowledge movement to include relatively more conservative figures and authors while excluding ones more squarely focused on emancipation.

14. See Pierre Bourdieu and Jean Claude Passeron, *Reproduction in Education, Society, and Culture,* 2nd ed., Thousand Oaks, CA: Sage, 1990. For a very concise explanation of the forms of capital see Pierre Bourdieu, "The Forms of Capital," pp. 46–58 in J. Richardson (ed.), *Handbook of Theory and Research for the Sociology of Education,* trans. Richard Nice, New York: Greenwood, 1986.

15. Bourdieu explains how class privilege is transmitted and inherited through both the transmission of monetary capital from parents to children, which might buy children into private elite schools, and social capital or social networks. As well, cultural capital involves distributing to children the means for appropriating socially valued knowledge, tastes, and dispositions. Why, for example, do the children of professional-class people find it second nature to learn about what appears in school books and hangs on the walls of museums? Such knowledge, tastes, and dispositions are rewarded in schools while the knowledge, tastes, and dispositions of working-class and poor students are punished in schools. Such seemingly neutral mechanisms as testing appear to reward hard work and talent when in fact, as Bourdieu explains, things that sanctify and exacerbate class privilege or exclusion begin in the home. The three forms of capital are exchangeable in various ways.

16. See Henry A. Giroux, *Theory and Resistance in Education,* Westport, CT: Bergin and Garvey, 1983; and Stanley Aronowitz and Henry Giroux, *Education Still Under Siege,* Westport, CT: Bergin and Garvey, 1989.

17. See Theodor Adorno, *Introduction to Sociology,* Stanford, CA: Polity Press, 2000.

18. For an excellent discussion of the need to retain the emancipatory elements of modernism while appropriating the best elements of postmodernism see Henry Giroux, "Rethinking the Boundaries of Educational Discourse: Modernism, Postmodernism,

and Feminism," in *Pedagogy and the Politics of Hope: Theory, Culture, and Schooling*, New York: Westview, 1994.

19. See Nancy Fraser, "From Discipline to Flexibilization? Rereading Foucault in the Shadow of Globalization," *Constellations* 10, 2 (2003), pp. 160–171.

20. The panopticon to use the gaze of surveillance to induce prisoners to regulate themselves was devised by Jeremy Bentham. See Michel Foucault's elaboration on the panopticon and the expansion of the technology of surveillance in education and other fields in *Discipline and Punish*. On the argument that the panoptic gaze is increasingly irrelevant as raw power controls bodies see on the syopticon Bauman's important discussion of California's super-max Pelican Bay prison in Zygmunt Bauman, *Globalization: The Human Consequences*, New York: Polity Press, 2000.

21. For details and a textual analysis of the rigid Success for All reading pedagogy see Kenneth J. Saltman, *The Edison Schools: Corporate Schooling and the Assault on Public Education*, New York: Routledge, 2005. Diane Ravitch celebrates the rigid approach of KIPP in *The Death and Life of the Great American School*. Here she admires the firm handshake and steady eye contact demanded of poor minority students, suggesting that such forms of physical control are the ticket to economic inclusion and academic success. Repeating a colonial educational trope and consistent with her nostalgia for pre–civil rights public education, this affirmation of corporeal coercion should be seen as centrally related to Ravitch's neoconservative view of culture that demands assimilation to a Euro-centric and conservative canon held to be of universal value and that allegedly represents the interests and histories of everyone. At the core of such approaches is submission and docility to powerful groups and institutions and their traditions rather than education as a practice of freedom and dissent in the critical pedagogical tradition.

22. See Joel Bakan, *Childhood Under Siege*, New York: Free Press, 2011. The current rampant uses of pharmacology to self-administer educational competition dosing can be found in a *60 Minutes* segment, "Boosting Brain Power," April 25, 2010, available at www.cbsnews.com/video/watch/?id-6430949n&tag-contentBody;storyMediaBox.

23. See Stanley Aronowitz, *Against Schooling: For an Education that Matters*, Boulder, CO: Paradigm, 2007.

24. Mark Fisher, *Capitalist Realism: Is There No Alternative?* Washington, DC: Zero Books, 2009. Fisher writes that capitalist realism "is more like a pervasive atmosphere, conditioning not only the production of culture but also the regulation of work and education, and acting as a kind of invisible barrier constraining thought and action" (p. 16).

25. This has been noted, for example, in Chapter 1, endnote 20. On the higher administrative cost of charters see G. Miron and J. L. Urschel, *Equal or Fair? A Study of Revenues and Expenditure in American Charter Schools*, Boulder, CO, and Tempe, AZ: Education and the Public Interest Center and Education Policy Research Unit, 2010, retrieved May 9, 2011, from http://epicpolicy.org/publication/charter-school -finance.

26. The centrality of context and student experience to critical pedagogy can be found elaborated in, for example, Paulo Freire, *Pedagogy of the Oppressed*, and in a number of

books by Henry Giroux, including *Theory and Resistance in Education, Border Crossings,* and *Teachers as Intellectuals.*

27. Thomas L. Friedman, "The New Untouchables," *New York Times,* October 21, 2009, p. A31.

28. See Kenneth Saltman, *The Gift of Education: Public Education and Venture Philanthropy,* New York: Palgrave Macmillan, 2010.

29. I detail this as the "circuit of privatization" in *The Gift of Education.*

30. Pierre Bourdieu and Jean Claude Passeron, *Reproduction in Education, Society, and Culture,* 2nd ed., Thousand Oaks, CA: Sage, 1990.

31. David Bornstein, "Coming Together to Give Schools a Boost," *New York Times,* March 7, 2011, available at http://opinionator.blogs.nytimes.com/2011/03/07/coming-together-to-give-schools-a-boost/.

32. For a plethora of research reviews that reveal the extent to which ideologically driven data manipulation is employed by corporate school reform ideologues, see the National Education Policy Center Think Tank Review Project, available at http://nepc.colorado.edu/think-tank-review-project. See, for example, R. L. Pecheone and R. C. Wei, *Review of "The Widget Effect: Our National Failure to Acknowledge and Act on Teacher Differences,"* Boulder, CO, and Tempe, AZ: Education and the Public Interest Center and Education Policy Research Unit, 2009, retrieved from http://epicpolicy.org/thinktank/review-Widget-Effect. For deception by Hanushek, see also J. Kilpatrick, *Review of "U.S. Math Performance in Global Perspective: How Well Does Each State Do at Producing High-Achieving Students?"* Boulder, CO: National Education Policy Center, 2011, retrieved from http://nepc.colorado.edu/thinktank/review-us-math. For deception by Finn, see W. S. Barnett, *Special Review of "Reroute the Preschool Juggernaut,"* Boulder, CO, and Tempe, AZ: Education and the Public Interest Center and Education Policy Research Unit, 2009, retrieved from http://epicpolicy.org/thinktank/Special-Review-Reroute-Preschool-Juggernaut. And for a nice example of deception by Peterson, see C. and S. Lubienski, *Review of "On the Public-Private School Achievement Debate,"* Boulder, CO, and Tempe, AZ: Education and the Public Interest Center and Education Policy Research Unit, 2006, retrieved from http://epicpolicy.org/thinktank/review-on-public-private-school-achievement-debate.

33. M. Fisher, *Capitalist Realism: Is There No Alternative?* London: John Hunt, 2009, p. 42.

34. Ibid., pp. 43–44.

35. See Theodor Adorno, *Introduction to Sociology,* Stanford, CA: Polity Press, 2000.

36. Both the Gates and Broad foundations have massively funded various forms of privatization, especially chartering but also database tracking projects to measure student test scores and teacher "performance" relative to the scores. When the charters were not showing promise on raising the test scores Gates shifted the criteria to focus on graduation rates and college enrollment rates. Similarly for CRPE's Paul Hill the standardized test scores should be used to justify closing traditional public schools but not for evaluating the contractors who take their place.

37. See Vivek Wadhwa, "U.S. Schools Are Still Ahead—Way Ahead," *Businessweek,* January 12, 2011, available at www.businessweek.com.

38. Alan Murray, "The End of Management," *Wall Street Journal,* August 21, 2010, available at www.wsj.com.

39. Charles Murray, "Why Charter Schools Fail the Test," *New York Times,* May 5, 2010, p. A31.

40. P. Hill, C. Campbell, and D. Menefee-Libey, *Portfolio School Districts for Big Cities: An Interim Report,* Seattle: Center on Reinventing Public Education, University of Washington, 2009.

41. This way of thinking about difference as needing to be registered in order to overcome such difference can be found exemplified in the speaking and writing of Vickie Philips, head of the Bill and Melinda Gates Foundation, and in books such as Abigail Thernstrom and Stephen Thernstrom, *No Excuses: Closing the Racial Gap in Learning,* New York: Simon and Shuster, 2003. Racial, ethnic, linguistic, and cultural difference is positioned in this discourse of the "achievement gap" as an obstacle and sometimes as a pathology that needs to be overcome. The way to overcome difference is to enforce the learning of prescribed knowledge that is alleged to be of universal value. This is diametrically opposed to critical pedagogy, in which difference needs to be engaged for how individuals and groups are positioned materially and symbolically in subordinate or superordinate ways and how such social positioning informs the claims to truth made by different parties. Such critical interrogations of difference form the basis for reconstructing individual and group experience and ideally form the basis for collective action toward equality.

42. For an excellent historical account of the political struggles over standardized testing see Mark J. Garrison, *A Measure of Failure: The Political Origins of Standardized Testing,* Albany, NY: SUNY Press, 2009. For an excellent contemporary take on the relationships between standardized testing and neoliberalism see David Hursh, *High-Stakes Testing and the Decline of Teaching and Learning,* Lanham, MD: Rowman and Littlefield, 2008. See also *The Nature and Limits of Standard-Based Reform and Assessment,* Sandra Mathison and E. Wayne Ross (eds), New York: Teachers College Press, 2008.

43. My book *The Gift of Education: Public Education and Venture Philanthropy,* New York: Palgrave Macmillan, 2010, details this largely ignored radical market-based transformation of educational philanthropy.

44. See Paulo Freire, *Pedagogy of the Oppressed,* New York: Continuum, 1970; Pierre Bourdieu and Jean Passeron, *Reproduction in Education, Society, and Culture,* Thousand Oaks, CA: Sage, 1990; and Bertell Ollman, "Why So Many Exams? A Marxist Response," *Z Magazine,* October 2002, available at www.nyu.edu/projects/ollman/docs/why_exams.php.

45. See Patricia Burch, *Hidden Markets: The New Educational Privatization,* New York: Routledge, 2009.

46. For-profit real estate investment cashing in on the charter boom includes numerous banks and corporations (Intel, movie companies) and even celebrity athletes

like Andre Agassi. See, for example, Tierney Plumb (The Motley Fool), "Movie House Investor Dives into Charter School Space," *Daily Finance,* August 16, 2011, available at www.dailyfinance.com/2011/08/16/movie-house-investor-dives-into-the-charter-school/; and Roger Vincent, "Agassi to Invest in Charter Schools," *Los Angeles Times,* June 2, 2011, available at http://articles.latimes.com/2011/jun/02/business/la-fi-agassi-fund-20110602.

47. According to the National Center for Children in Poverty, 15 million, or 21 percent, of U.S. children live below the poverty line. See www.nccp.org/topics/childpoverty .html. According to the campaign to end childhood homelessness 1.5 million U.S. children are homeless. That is, 1 in 50, or 2 percent, of American children are homeless. See www.homelesschildrenamerica.org/.

Chapter Four

1. By *critical* here I mean that the criticism of corporatization has been centrally focused on its implication in broader systemic and structural power struggles. Some extremely valuable liberal criticisms of corporate school reform, including those of Jonathan Kozol, Dorothy Shipps, Patricia Burch, Jeffrey Henig, Richard Rothstein, and Henry Levin, have avoided linking these initiatives to interrogating the ways that, for example, capitalism, liberal electoral democracy in its current incarnation, and existing cultural formations produce extreme inequalities, violence and oppression, and injustice. Challenging the corporate takeover of public education cannot be about merely defending the existing social order but rather must be the basis for reconstructing it.

2. Diane Ravitch, *The Death and Life of the Great American School,* Boston: Beacon, 2010; and Linda Darling-Hammond, *The Flat World and Education,* New York: Teachers College Press, 2010, do a good job of compiling the empirical evidence of the failure of numerous corporate reforms on their own terms. An indispensable resource on charters, EMOs, and commercialism is the research conducted by the National Education Policy Center (much of which is cited in endnotes below), available at www.nepc.colorado.edu.

3. See Chapter 1, endnote 20, for studies on charter school effects on academic achievement.

4. Charter and EMO racial segregation studies: Gary Miron, Jessica L. Urschel, William Mathis, and Elana Tornquist, "Schools Without Diversity: Education Management Organizations, Charter Schools, and the Demographic Stratification of the American School System," Great Lakes Center for Education Research & Practice, February 2010, available at www.greatlakescenter.org; Erica Frankenberg, Genevieve Siegel-Hawley, and Jia Wang, "Choice Without Equity: Charter School Segregation and the Need for Civil Rights Standards," January 2010, the Civil Rights Project, available at www.civilrightsproject.ucla.edu.

5. Henry A. Giroux, "Chartering Disaster: Why Duncan's Corporate-Based Schools Can't Deliver an Education That Matters," t r u t h o u t, June 21, 2010. See Gary Miron and Jessica L. Urschel, *Equal or Fair? A Study of Revenues and Expenditures in American*

Charter Schools, Boulder, CO, and Tempe, AZ: Education and the Public Interest Center and Education Policy Research Unit, retrieved March 13, 2011, from http://epicpolicy .org/publication/charter-school-finance.

6. Paul Thomas, "The Corporate Takeover of America's Schools," *Guardian* (UK), November 16, 2010, available at www.commondreams.org; Henry A. Giroux, op-ed, "Selling Out New York City's Public Schools: Mayor Bloomberg, David Steiner, and the Politics of Corporate 'Leadership,'" t r u t h o u t, December 7, 2010; Henry A. Giroux, op-ed, "Lessons to Be Learned from Paulo Freire as Education Is Being Taken Over by the Mega Rich," t r u t h o u t, November 23, 2010; Henry A. Giroux, op-ed, "Business Culture and the Death of Public Education: The Triumph of Management Over Leadership," t r u t h o u t, November 12, 2010.

7. That charter reliance on philanthropic support that can dry up seems to be agreed upon across the political spectrum: see, for example, P. Hill, C. Campbell, and D. Menefee-Libey, *Portfolio School Districts for Big Cities: An Interim Report,* Seattle: Center on Reinventing Public Education, University of Washington, 2009; and Kenneth J. Saltman, "Urban School Decentralization and the Growth of 'Portfolio Districts,'" *Great Lakes Center for Education Research and Practice,* June 2010, available at www .greatlakescenter.org. See also my extended discussion of venture philanthropy in education in *The Gift of Education: Public Education and Venture Philanthropy,* New York: Palgrave Macmillan, 2010.

8. For a recent celebration of "churn" or "creative destruction," see A. Smarick, "The Turnaround Fallacy," *Education Next* 10, 1 (2010), available at http://educationnext .org/the-turnaround-fallacy/. Smarick suggests that the "advantage" of charter schools is that they can be easily closed and replaced with other privatized solutions. For a clear example of "churn" or "creative destruction" in the context of the portfolio district model see P. Hill, C. Campbell, and D. Menefee-Libey, *Portfolio School Districts for Big Cities: An Interim Report,* Seattle: Center on Reinventing Public Education, University of Washington, 2009, p. 1: "In a portfolio district, schools are not assumed to be permanent but contingent.... A portfolio district is built for continuous improvement via expansion and imitation of the highest-performing schools, closure and replacement of the lowest-performing, and constant search for new ideas." I criticize these positions in Kenneth J. Saltman, "Urban School Decentralization and the Growth of 'Portfolio Districts,'" *Great Lakes Center for Education Research and Practice,* June 2010, available at www.greatlakescenter.org.

9. See Gary Miron and Jessica L. Urschel, *Equal or Fair? A Study of Revenues and Expenditures in American Charter Schools,* Boulder, CO, and Tempe, AZ: Education and the Public Interest Center and Education Policy Research Unit, retrieved March 13, 2011, from http://epicpolicy.org/publication/charter-school-finance.

10. "Interview with Federal Reserve Chairman Ben Bernanke," *60 Minutes,* December 5, 2010, available at www.cbsnews.com/8301-504803_162-20024635-10391709.html.

11. "Correspondent Steve Kroft Interviewed the President," *60 Minutes,* November 4, 2010, available at www.cbsnews.com/stories/2010/11/07/60minutes/main7032276_ page5.shtml?tag-contentMain;contentBody.

12. Thomas L. Friedman, "The New Untouchables," *New York Times,* October 20, 2009, available at www.nytimes.com.

13. Henry A. Giroux, "In Defense of Public School Teachers in a Time of Crisis," t r u t h o u t, April 14, 2010, available at www.truthout.org.

14. Alan Murray, "The End of Management," *Wall Street Journal,* August 21, 2010, available at www.wsj.com.

15. While many neoliberals and liberals alike add the need for citizenship to the economic rationale for public schooling, inevitably this turns into the tell-tale term "making productive citizens," belying the conflation of civic participation with economic activity and positioning education for citizenship as both secondary to the economic and defining citizenship through inclusion into existing exclusionary and corporate-dominated institutions (like an electoral system beholden to campaign contributions and media advertising and a legislature beholden to corporate lobbying).

16. Linda Darling-Hammond in *The Flat World and Education,* New York: Teachers College Press, 2010, does call for desegregating and equalizing funding, but as I discuss below it is toward the end of a neoliberal economism that can never achieve economic and racial justice on either a national or global scale.

17. Sharon Schmidt, "Diane Ravitch Stirs Overflow Crowd in CTU Lecture," *Substance News,* March 13, 2011, www.substancenews.net.

18. One of the few left criticisms of postconversion Ravitch is by Rich Gibson, "Against Ravitch," *Substance News,* March 23, 2010, www.substancenews.net. Gibson writes, "What makes Ravitch consistent—and consistently reactionary—is her dishonest rejection of the social context of the NCLB and its monster sibling, The Race to the Top (RATT), that is, her utter failure to locate these regimented education moves with the continuing crises of the system of capital, today losing wars and forging booming inequality." Although Gibson is right, his tendency for class reductionism leaves him with an impoverished theory of culture as a mere reflection and effect of overdetermining relations of capital, which makes theorizing agency and engaging in cultural work for systemic change challenging.

19. Susan Ohanian, "Betrayal: The Common Core, Liberals, NCTE, BYOB, and the Media," *Substance News,* March 9, 2011, www.substancenews.net.

20. Henry A. Giroux, *The Giroux Reader,* pp. 185–186.

21. As Stanley Aronowitz has contended in his book *Against Schooling: For An Education that Matters,* Boulder, CO: Paradigm, 2008, the labor movement needs to revisit its critical intellectual roots.

22. *Democracy Now!* featured Ravitch four times in 2010: "Obama Defends Sweeping Education Reforms in Face of Criticism from Minority and Teachers' Groups," July 30, 2010; "Part II: Leading Education Scholar Diane Ravitch on 'The Death and Life of the Great American School System,'" March 8, 2010; blog post "Amy Goodman and Juan Gonzalez Interviewed Diane Ravitch in the *Democracy Now!* Studios Last Week," available at www.democracynow.org/2010/3/5/protests; and "Leading Education Scholar Diane Ravitch: No Child Left Behind Has Left US Schools with Legacy of 'Institutionalized Fraud,'" March 5, 2010.

23. Ravitch appeared in 2010 alone in *The Nation* as author, subject of stories, video interview on Nation-produced GritTV, and book review subject. See www .thenation.com/search/apachesolr_search/diane%20ravitch?filters=created%3A[2010-01 -01T00%3A00%3A00Z%20TO%202011-01-01T00%3A00%3A00Z].

24. To its credit, *Democracy Now!* has put critical education scholar/activist Lois Weiner on the air.

25. Henry A. Giroux, "Disposable Youth and the Politics of Domestic Militarization," in *The Giroux Reader*, ed. Christopher Robbins, Boulder, CO: Paradigm, 2006, pp. 169–170.

26. Linda Darling-Hammond, *The Flat World and Education*, New York: Teachers College Press, 2010.

27. Ibid.

28. For a small sample of Giroux's discussion of the relationship between culture and economy in the context of theorizing education and other cultural work, see Stanley Aronowitz and Henry A. Giroux, *Education Still Under Siege*, Westport, CT: Bergin and Garvey, 1989; Henry A. Giroux, *Disturbing Pleasures*, New York: Routledge, 1992; Henry A. Giroux, *Border Crossings: Cultural Workers and the Politics of Education*, 2nd ed., New York: Routledge, 2005; and Henry A. Giroux, *Impure Acts: The Practical Politics of Cultural Studies*, New York: Routledge, 2000.

29. See Henry A. Giroux, *Theory and Resistance in Education*, Westport, CT: Bergin and Garvey, 1983; and Henry A. Giroux, *Pedagogy and the Politics of Hope*, Chapter 1, "Schooling and the Culture of Positivism: Notes on the Death of History," and Chapter 2, "Culture and Rationality in Frankfurt School Thought: Ideological Foundations for a Theory of Social Education," New York: Westview, 1997.

30. Thomas L. Friedman, *The Lexus and the Olive Tree*, New York: Anchor Books, 2000. For an extended discussion of Friedman's neoliberal thought in relation to education and culture, see Robin Truth Goodman and Kenneth J. Saltman, *Strange Love, or How We Learn to Stop Worrying and Love the Market*, Lanham, MD: Rowman and Littlefield, 2002.

31. Henry A. Giroux, *The Giroux Reader*, pp. 183–184.

32. See Henry A. Giroux, *Teachers as Intellectuals: Toward a Critical Pedagogy of Learning*, Westport, CT: Bergin and Garvey, 1988.

Chapter Five

1. On the hijacking of the language of social justice by neoliberal education, one can find this repeatedly in the speeches of U.S. Secretary of Education Arne Duncan. I heard Duncan equate privatization initiatives with efforts for social justice at the Commercial Club of Chicago's Renaissance Schools Fund "Free to Choose, Free to Succeed: The New Market in Public Education" event in Chicago on May 6, 2008. See, for example, "Secretary of Education Arne Duncan's 'Call to Service Lecture at Harvard University,'" available at the U.S. Department of Education website, www.ed.gov/news/speeches/

call-service-lecture-harvard-university. For criticism of this misuse of the language of social justice in education see, for example, Henry Giroux, *Education and the Crisis of Public Values,* New York: Peter Lang, 2011.

2. Despite the long critical educational tradition in the United States, ranging from the reconstructionists to critical pedagogy, most progressive magazines—such as *The Nation* and *Harper's*—tend to largely exclude the critical education perspective, instead promoting either liberal or activist views.

3. Tooley has also authored a book framing feminism as a threat to women globally: James Tooley, *The Mis-Education of Women,* Chicago: Ivan R. Dee, 2003. Tooley's position that women's place is in the home and that feminism threatens masculine domination of the economy should be taken seriously in relation to his call for a corporate fast food model of education in poor countries. He demonstrates a consistent commitment to inequality that spans economic class and gender. That the World Bank has so aggressively embraced Tooley's "scholarship" should not come as that great of a surprise to those familiar with the World Bank's history of imposing debt servitude, privatization, and other aspects of "structural adjustment" on poor nations while helping to enrich private interests in rich nations.

4. Positivist rationality was thoroughly criticized by the members of the Frankfurt School of Critical Theory, including Theodor Adorno, Max Horkheimer, and Herbert Marcuse. In education Henry Giroux and Stanley Aronowitz stand out for their use of critical theory to apply the criticism to school policy and reform.

5. See Zygmunt Bauman, *The Individualized Society,* Malden, MA: Blackwell, 2001.

6. Linda Darling-Hammond, *The Flat World and Education,* New York: Teachers College, Press 2010, p. 28.

7. Ibid., p. 26.

8. Stanley Aronowitz, *Against Schooling: For an Education that Matters,* Boulder: Paradigm, 2008.

9. On the need for an intertwined theory of economic distribution and cultural recognition see Nancy Fraser, *Justice Interruptus,* New York: Routledge, 1997, particularly Chapters 1 and 3, and the more recent *Scales of Justice,* New York: Columbia, 2009, in which she expands the economic and cultural matrix to include political representation.

10. See, for example, Jonathan Kozol, *The Shame of the Nation,* New York: Three Rivers Press, 2005.

11. See Nancy Fraser, *Scales of Justice,* New York: Columbia, 2009.

12. Nancy Fraser, "From Discipline to Flexibilization: Rereading Foucault in the Shadow of Globalization," *Constellations* 10, 2 (2003), p. 166.

13. Some scholars have turned to what I have previously criticized in *The Gift of Education* as the "new old Marxism," which puts a valuable emphasis on class yet destructively positions other traditions as the enemy of the one "pure" discourse. Marx continues to offer crucial insights, but the return to vulgar Marxism in education repeats some of the worst aspects of the Marxist tradition, including especially vangardism and this quasi-religious discourse of purity.

14. See Georges Batailles, *The Accursed Share, Volume One*, New York: Zone Books, 1995. Jean Baudrillard, *The Consumer Society*, Thousand Oaks, CA: Sage, 1998, was an important early work that recognized this, and more recently Zygmunt Bauman, *Wasted Lives: Modernity and Its Outcasts*, Cambridge, UK: Polity Press, 2004, and Henry Giroux, *Youth in a Suspect Society*, New York: Palgrave Macmillan, 2010, have made important interventions. Giroux's book significantly links the death of futurity signified in the ramped up hard and soft war on youth to the dead end of consumer capitalism and ecological disaster. See also Alex Means, "Neoliberalism and the Politics of Disposability: Education, Urbanization, and Displacement in the New Chicago," *Journal of Critical Education Policy Studies* 6, 1 (2008).

15. See Richard Wolff's important film "Capitalism Hits the Fan" (2008) produced by Media Education Foundation.

16. Slavoj Zizek, *First as Tragedy, Then as Farce*, New York: Verso, 2009, p. 91.

17. Ibid.

18. David Harvey, "The Future of the Commons," *Radical History Review* (Winter 2011), p. 105.

19. Ibid.

20. See Linda Darling-Hammond, *The Flat World and Education*, New York: Teachers College Press, 2010, for abundant empirical evidence as to the destructive effects of these antiteacher policies on the "quality" of teaching as measured by test outputs.

21. By critically engaged I am referring not to critical thinking as problem solving skills but rather critical in the tradition of critical pedagogy, which takes up questions of knowledge in relation to broader power struggles, interests, and social structures.

22. Lois Weiner, *The Global Assault on Teaching, Teachers, and Their Unions*, New York: Palgrave Macmillan, 2008.

23. See the Bill and Melinda Gates Foundation website, www.gatesfoundation.org/college-ready-education/Pages/default.aspx The website posts a "Featured Fact" that nicely illustrates the assumption that higher education produces economic opportunity: "Featured Fact: By 2018, 63 percent of all American job openings will require some sort of postsecondary education." The significance of this "featured fact" is that it suggests that by preparing individuals for higher education, secondary education is creating economic opportunities. This is fallacious in that the education itself does not create greater levels of employment or affect the unemployment rate or cause expansion or contraction in industries. See also Secretary of Education Arne Duncan's "Call to Service Lecture at Harvard University," available on the U.S. Department of Education website at www.ed.gov/news/speeches/call-service-lecture-harvard-university.

24. Arne Duncan put it succinctly shortly before praising the propaganda film *Waiting for Superman*: "As President Obama says, education is one of the best antipoverty programs." See Duncan's "Call to Service Lecture at Harvard University," www.ed.gov/news/speeches/call-service-lecture-harvard-university.

25. Rick Perry claimed a Texas miracle in job creation while he was governor, while Mitt Romney countered that Perry created those jobs by luring people from other

states (which wouldn't be an option for the U.S. president). An excellent exposé on the state-to-state theft of jobs that are then attributed to elected officials can be found in *This American Life* episode 435, "How to Create a Job," originally aired May 13, 2011, available at www.thisamericanlife.org/radio-archives/episode/435/how-to-create-a-job.

26. David Harvey, "The Future of the Commons," *Radical History Review* (Winter 2011), p. 107.

27. Louis Althusser, "Ideology and Ideological State Apparatuses: Notes Towards an Investigation," in *Mapping Ideology*, ed. Slavoj Zizek, New York: Verso, 1994 [orig. 1969–1970], p. 111.

28. Ibid., p. 119.

29. Ibid., p. 119.

30. See Edward Herman and Noam Chomsky, *Manufacturing Consent*, New York: Pantheon, 1988, and the work of Robert W. McChesney, such as *Rich Media, Poor Democracy*.

31. G. Miron, J. L. Urschel, W. J. Mathis, and E. Tornquist, *Schools Without Diversity: Education Management Organizations, Charter Schools, and the Demographic Stratification of the American School System*, Boulder, CO, and Tempe, AZ: Education and the Public Interest Center and Education Policy Research Unit, 2010, retrieved from http://epicpolicy.org/publication/schools-without-diversity.

INDEX

ABOUT THE AUTHOR

Dr. Kenneth J. Saltman is a professor in the Educational Policy Studies and Research Department and the Social and Cultural Foundations in Education graduate program at DePaul University. He is the author most recently of *The Gift of Education: Public Education and Venture Philanthropy* (Palgrave Macmillan 2010), which was awarded a 2011 American Educational Studies Critics Choice Book Award; *Capitalizing on Disaster: Taking and Breaking Public Schools* (Paradigm 2007), which was awarded a 2008 American Educational Studies Critics Choice Book Award; and *The Edison Schools: Corporate Schooling and the Assault on Public Education* (Routledge 2005). His recent edited collections include *Education as Enforcement: The Militarization and Corporatization of Schools*, 2nd Edition, with David Gabbard (Routledge 2010), *Schooling and the Politics of Disaster* (Routledge 2007), and *The Critical Middle School Reader*, with Enora Brown (Routledge 2005). He received a Fulbright Scholarship in 2006 on Globalization and Culture and is a fellow of the National Education Policy Center.